AFTER DARK

PARANORMAL INVESTIGATIONS
TRUE CASES OF THE NTPARANORMAL TEAM

WRITTEN BY
ASHTON ROGERS

CO-AUTHORS
ALLIE BOLTON
SARA HATFIELD
KRISTIN MARTINDALE

After Dark Paranormal Investigations © 2018 by Ashton Rogers. All Rights Reserved.

All rights reserved. No part of this book may be reproduced in any form or by any electronic or mechanical means including information storage and retrieval systems, without permission in writing from the author. The only exception is by a reviewer, who may quote short excerpts in a review.

Cover designed by Ashton Rogers
Cover Photo by Donald Cook

Ashton Rogers
Visit my website at https://www.amazon.com/Ashton-Rogers

Printed in the United States of America

First Printing: Feb 2018
Amazon Printing

ISBN-9781976966972

DEDICATION

This book is dedicated to those who experienced something profound, but didn't tell anyone because they thought they would not be believed. Also, for my dad. If you're still out there, it would be nice to hear your voice one more time.

TABLE OF CONTENTS

PARANORMAL SCIENCE: A CONTRADICTION	1
YOUR HOUSE "PROBABLY ISN'T HAUNTED	15
ELECTROMAGNETIC FREQUENCIES	18
ELECTRONIC VOICE PHENOMENON	21
PHOTOGRAPHY AND VIDEO	28
THE FIRST EXPERIENCE	37
ON THE JOB TRAINING: ASHTON ROGERS	40
A LIFE OF ADAPTATION: SARA HATFIELD	53
THE GREEN HOUSE: KRISTIN MARTINDALE	67
WHAT'S THAT SOUND?: ALLIE BOLTON	80
THE CASES OF NTPARANORMAL	90
"DON'T RUN" : ANTIOCH REST CEMETERY	93
BORED TO DEATH: THE CARTERSVILLE GHOST TOWN	111
SCHRÖDINGERS'S HAUNTING: THE ARLINGTON VISITOR CENTER	126
THIS WAY TO THE GOATMAN: ALTON BRIDGE	140
SINCE TEXAS BECAME TEXAS: HOLDER ESTATE	156
WHY IS IT ALWAYS DOLLS? : A.W.PERRY HOMESTEAD MUSEUM	176
LEAVING THE GATE OPEN: KYLE CEMETERY AND HAMM CREEK	192
OBJECTIVE BELIEF	221

ACKNOWLEDGMENTS

Thank you to the friends and family in my life who support and encourage me to write. Without your constant encouragement, pushing, and eagerness to read what I put to paper, I would never get anything done.

Special thanks to my NTParanormal family who helped me with their contributions, support, and willingness to put up with me for so long. I may not always be the easiest person to work with. But, I am always *right*.

NTPARANORMAL INVESTIGATIONS

NTParanormal is a group of paranormal researchers based out of Fort Worth, Texas. It is their goal to study paranormal activity using the scientific method, experiments, and documentation, in an attempt, to prove or disprove the existence of currently unexplained supernatural phenomenon in the locations that they are called to investigate, mainly in the North Texas region. NTParanormal investigates both residential and public locations on a regular basis, participates in larger studies and field research when available. They have strived to help people who are looking for answers about paranormal phenomenon in their homes or businesses with the intent to educate about the suspected activity in question.

NTParanormal Investigations was started in 2013 by Ashton Rogers, Allie Bolton, and Sara Hatfield. Since then, they have participated in over a hundred investigations and case studies.

All audio and video related to the cases and evidence presented in this book can be found at the NTPI website, along with more information about NTPI.

Website: www.ntparanormal.com
Facebook: facebook.com/ntparanormal

PARANORMAL SCIENCE
A CONTRADICTION

Put ten people in a room with me and I'll show you three in that group who already believe in ghosts. After that, I'll show you three more who I will convince that the paranormal is not only real but something that can be proven with science. Finally, from that same group I can produce yet another three, who although don't think that anything presented by me proves the existence of the paranormal, will tell you I'm not insane, nor stupid, and that my experiences are valid. That last person in the room, if you have done your math, doesn't believe anything I've told them. They think I'm an idiot and had their mind made up from the start. There's not much I can do about that person even if I show them definitive evidence.

In 2014, Gallup took a poll showing that in the United States, that roughly one-third of the country believes in ghosts. Expand that poll out to include angels, aliens, lizard people, and other paranormal phenomenon and you might be surprised to find that the total number is closer to about seventy to ninety percent. Whether we want to admit it or not, our instinct is to believe that there is more going on under the surface of our world than what meets the eye. We are a society that believes in evil spells, alien abductions, and a host of conspiracies even though, on the outside, we like to project ourselves as rational beings of dignified science and logic.

The words paranormal and science often get thrown together and go hand in hand. But, they are quite contradictory to each other. Let's take a quick peek at the official definitions of both:

> **Science (Noun)** - The intellectual and practical activity encompassing the systematic study of the structure and behavior of the physical and natural world through observation and experiment.

> **Paranormal (Adj)** - Denoting events or phenomena such as telekinesis or clairvoyance that are beyond the scope of normal scientific understanding.

This means that the idea of Paranormal Science is a bit of an oxymoron. Clark's third law states that Any sufficiently advanced technology is indistinguishable from magic. We can adapt this thinking to our case, in that, anything that we do not currently understand we will consider paranormal and fantastic. Once we use science to confirm a paranormal event, you are removing the part of it that is paranormal. As soon as it becomes explainable by science, it just becomes normal.

Even the most respected scientists in the world will tell you that they initially became interested in their fields because of some mystical allure of forbidden knowledge that could be learned through the mediumship of science. No ten-year-old child ever set out to become a microbiologist because they wanted to test milk cultures at a dairy plant for $12.00 an hour. No, when they set out on their path, they were looking for aliens and the fanciful.

While that may be true for most scientists, it's doubly true for anyone who claims themselves to be a paranormal investigator. Usually, "ghost hunting" is not a field you fall into while studying something else more prestigious at MIT. Most parapsychologists and investigators start off with a preconceived notion of belief and try to take it a step further by validating what they think they already know with science. Unfortunately, the results are a bit of a mixed bag. This irrational notion of armchair scientists and pseudoscience disciples planting the proverbial flag on the north pole of paranormal activity is mostly a childish fantasy. Many of us in the field are considered quintessential sci-fi nerd fans that just never grew up. And honestly, as a member of that culture, I couldn't agree more with that observation.

Over the years I have been doing this, paranormal investigation has seen a huge uptick in popularity across the globe. So much so, that it is reminiscent of the spiritualist movement of the eighteen hundred's. We're seeing in a world of modern marvels, science, and technology a huge resurgence of interest in the paranormal. Most of this, I believe, is due to the digital age. It's easier for the average person to get their material out there to be viewed by the masses and it's certainly more affordable than ever to get your hands-on instrumentation now with only a few mouse clicks. Our senses are constantly bombarded with an assortment of ghost hunter shows, ghost hunting equipment shops online, and thousands of ghost hunting groups all over the world. It's now becoming harder than ever to sort all the fact from fiction.

But, as much as it pains me to say so, maybe that's not an entirely bad thing. It's no secret that the world is becoming a tougher place to deal with. We're rapidly overpopulating, were running out of resources, and my generation is painfully finding that it's inheriting a world from the previous generation that, not only wasn't taken care of, but in some cases deliberately sabotaged for us out of spite. It's this new generation of people who are looking for any bit of light and encouragement that they can to help push them through some of the bleakness. So, if something as wondrous as the idea of the paranormal provides the mystery and narrative needed to keep that light burning, I can't be angry at that.

Modern ghost hunting is akin to ancient myth building. There's little in the world left to really amaze us and scratch that need for discovery. Our species can't survive without some sort of question to be answered. We're always striving to learn, grow, and build. This may be one of the reasons we continue to search for the answers to these unknowable things. Or, maybe it's because we're arrogant enough to think that there are no questions that we can't eventually answer if we're just persistent enough with the same tried and true (tired) techniques. It's not something I agree with. I feel like new ideas require new thinking and an open mind to recognize and accept new information, but without being blinded by totally fantastic possibilities.

As the lead investigator of NTParanormal Investigations, I wanted to write a book about the cases that we have taken on over the years. In that book, I wanted to present evidence and facts that would help convince people that the things we've seen over the years are not only real but scientifically valid. More than that, I wanted to write an honest book about the paranormal and our study of it. But, the cold hard reality of that is it may never be possible write that book. Our study is a study of the unknowable. Our conclusions, although informed, are still speculation at best. After years of cases, investigations, and experiments we are hardly any closer to a hard conclusion than we were when we started this whole crazy adventure. In fact, in true scientific fashion, we probably have more questions now than when we started. While frustrating, I have to say it's rather fitting.

Let's get some things perfectly clear before we continue. Paranormal investigation is pseudoscience. For most teams claiming to be legitimate, that's a dirty word. But, it's a cold sobering truth that I think is hard for many to swallow. Let's not ignore or deny that countless research teams, groups, and individuals have conducted experiments in ways that favor the conclusions that they wanted to see at the end of their study. Uncontrolled environments, mishandling of equipment, and poor understanding of data by haphazard researchers have all hurt the credibility of anyone else looking to do legitimate work in the field. Myself included when starting out, there is little place for a newcomer to find any information outside of the very groups who are causing the damage. Misinformation just breeds even more misinformation. I have yet to encounter any other investigation groups that don't claim to use science as the basis for their studies. Only later, for a good number of them, to tell me about the proof uncovered and documented by their groups resident psychic medium. Bombarded with a swath of reality ghost hunting television shows I feel like they are little more than paranormal soft-core pornography. Always promising to show you the proof of paranormal activity, only for it to be just out of frame or happening off camera.

The truth of the matter is that even if all groups are claiming to use science as the basis for their investigations, a great many of them are not. The fact is, in all the years of paranormal research, never once in the history of anything, ever, has anyone provided any solid scientific proof of ghosts, spirits, or paranormal phenomenon. I find it to be a knee-jerk reaction of most groups to claim the forefront of science as their basis of investigation to sound more credible just, so people will listen to what they have to say. However, go through any case, my own included, and I can point out the breaks in the chain of the scientific method that ultimately invalidates any of the presented evidence of being considered scientific proof. Having said that, I do not want to discredit the evidence and experience entirely. A common misconception is that evidence, experience, and proof are all the same thing. But, we're talking about very different concepts when we analyze what each of these things represents in an honest paranormal case. Let's break down fundamentally the differences of what each piece represents in the grand scheme of a study.

Personal experiences, by my own estimation, are about ninety-five percent of what keep people convinced that there are supernatural forces at work. Neither evidence or proof, but simply feelings or events that have happened to a person at one time or another are enough to convince them that there are things happening beyond our comprehension. Bumps in the night, paranoia, feelings of being attacked by an unseen force, or visits from dead relatives all rank among the most common reports. To the subject the event happened to, it's the most real experience they have ever had, profound enough to change their view of the world around them permanently. Even to the point, that when I can provide a completely logical explanation for the experience, many times that explanation is still challenged. But, does that make personal experiences any less valid knowing that your memories and senses can completely fabricate the whole thing? I don't think it does. While I could never list a personal experience as either evidence or proof of paranormal activity, I still feel that experience is still very valid, if not the most valid of the three.

The way we perceive the world around us is flawed. Our bodies and our senses are known to adapt to the world around us. Our body only gives us the information that is needed for survival. For example, after a long study of ancient texts, it was discovered that until more recent times in the human timeline we never had any written references to blue. It was speculated that because there was no necessity for anyone to see it, that our brains did not even process the information.

William Gladstone, while studying The Odyssey, would find that Homer described the ocean as "wine-dark" and other hues, but never in the entire text used the word 'blue'. Lazarus Geiger, would follow up on this by analyzing ancient Icelandic, Hindi, Chinese, Arabic and Hebrew texts, to find no mention of the color.

This discovery was a bit of a surprise, but made some since. Other than the sky, there isn't a lot in nature that is inherently blue. The first society in written history to have a word for the color were the Egyptians, the only culture that could produce dyes of that color.

But, just because there was no word for blue, does that mean our ancestors couldn't see it? Jules Davidoff, a psychologist from the Goldsmiths University of London worked with the Himba tribe from Namibia on a study to answer that question. In their writings, he found that in their language, there is no word for blue and no real distinction between green and blue.

To test whether that meant they couldn't see blue, he showed them a circle with eleven green squares and one obvious blue square. But, as predicted, the Himba tribe struggled to tell Davidoff which of the squares was a different color than the others. Moreover, when they showed a circle containing a square only a slightly different shade of green, they could pick it out immediately. I can imagine the first of the Himba tribesman who begins to recognize the hue and not being believed by the rest of his people. What an alienating experience to know of this new knowledge, use it to create a work of art or something else of value, only for the masses to discredit, not understand, or not appreciate the information being presented.

What this tells us about our senses and experiences is that, through selective filtering, they avoid giving us information that is not pertinent to our environment for survival even if the sensory input is there. Thus, when we're able to see something that we don't understand, perceiving it as paranormal would be our brain's way of telling us that there is something very important that we need to understand in the environment around us. It's this logic in my mind that makes "personal experience" still a valid part of the paranormal investigation. However, because senses are flawed and even prone to being completely wrong, they cannot be considered evidence or proof. It only tells us that an event happened, profound enough that your brain needed to inform you of the data, and that there was no other information at the time available to help you understand it.

Outside the field of science, evidence is often confused as proof. And, while the two go hand in hand, they are very different things. Evidence supports proof, but can never be a true substitute for the latter.

Imagine, if you will, a murder case. The prosecutor presents evidence in the case. There is a gun that we know was used to kill the victim and that gun was registered to the defendant; his handprints are on the gun, as well as a second set of prints and a receipt for ammunition a day before the crime was committed found at the defendant's house. This is certainly good evidence that the defendant committed the crime, but is it proof?

The defendant claims that while all the evidence is correct, that it was his brother who took his gun that killed the victim. After analyzing the second set of prints on the weapon and comparing them to his brother's, we find that there is a positive match. Now our evidence supports two separate theoretical conclusions. However, we know that at the end of the day there is only one truth. Based on that information alone, you could not convict one person or another because you would not have any proof either way. Based on that evidence alone, until eyewitness statements and several other pieces of evidence were entered into question could I come to even a speculation on who committed the crime.

Evidence supports proof. It tells us that something happened, it can tell us the mechanics involved, and likely course of actions. But, evidence is only a supporting factor to proof. Just because we may get an electromagnetic spike in a certain area of a supposedly haunted location, this is not proof of a paranormal event, but rather, several possible outcomes. Only after gathering more evidence over the course of an investigation and ruling out possible sources can we narrow down the choice of possible conclusions. Conclusions based on evidence alone are well-informed speculations, but still speculations at the end of the day. However, conclusions based on evidence and proof together are considered facts.

In our court case scenario, let's pretend that very clear security camera footage of the crime in progress is provided. Clear enough that the brother could be positively identified as the killer. A conviction at that point would hardly be a moral quandary in the least. It would be undeniable proof so profound that it could even standalone without the support of any other evidence. In fact, it would be so airtight, that even if one of the eyewitnesses swore they saw someone else at the time of the murder, you would question the validity of their account. Proof is such a profound fact that it can withstand the scrutiny of error. Proof is fact, and will yield the same result over and over without fail. It removes any question of a divergent outcome when the set conditions are met.

In my time of investigation, I have never personally found proof of the paranormal, nor has any other person in history before me. There is not one solitary shred of proof to be found out there that scientifically proves the existence of an afterlife, spirits, ghosts, or other such supernatural beings. However, there is legitimate evidence to be found if you look for it.

Another thing that should be painfully addressed is that there is not a common understanding or agreement of what is considered a ghost, spirit, demon, or any other number of specter related names. It's this inconsistency, I think, that contributes to the confusion and forbear of paranormal research. For the sake of our research, we do not usually try to differentiate any nomenclature that would separate a ghost from a spirit or demonic presence. For the sake of being objective, we do not insert our personal beliefs into the data that we collect. Although, when something feels profoundly negative and oppressive it's very hard not to paint that event in your mind as an interaction with something "demonic" in nature. However, as a case study, we typically will refer to the nature of activity in two categories: Intelligent Entities and Residual (non-intelligent).

Intelligent hauntings and activity are a relatively straightforward concept that most people can grasp readily and are, at least in my experience and ironically, less common if the two. I feel it is the standard model of thinking that comes to people's minds when they think of haunted houses and ghosts. The quintessential tragic death of someone ripped from the world too fast, they don't know they are dead and tragically wander wherever in search of a resolution to move on. Most people think of intelligent hauntings as spirits of the once living still wandering around the places they died looking for people to exclaim "Boo!" at. It's of note that almost all malevolent type hauntings will fall into this category as the entity would have to have an awareness to actively terrorize its victim. The entity in an intelligent haunting can interact, respond, manipulate the environment, is generally aware of their surroundings, and in some cases also aware of the fact that it does not exist in the same way that the investigators do.

While most people conjure up the idea of old Bob Cratchit and his chains, intelligent entities for us sweep a range of common models, but will always fall back to being something that we can interact with rather than just observe. In my personal experience, I don't feel like I've ever encountered an intelligent haunting with anything that was formerly human. I can honestly say I'm not entirely sure that Bob Cratchit is even a plausible scenario at this point in our studies.

Far more commonplace in our research, but less considered by the mainstream public, is the residual haunting. Whatever it is being observed makes noises, creates smells, and sometimes visually appears. However, in all its glory, never seems to interact with anyone or anything in the location that denotes any kind of awareness of the observer or its environment. It may give us responses in the form of electronic voice phenomenon, but the responses have no connection to any of the questions asked. These apparitions seem to have their own set routines and rules that are not dependent on any outside factors such as personal interaction or even building structure. Of course, there are many theories put forth by several people in the field, the most popular and well known being the Stone Tape Theory.

The Stone Tape theory is an idea that hauntings are much to the same degree as tape recordings, and that electrical mental impressions released during emotional or traumatic events can somehow be "stored" in the environments in which they happen. The idea was first put into the collective by British archaeologist turned parapsychologist Thomas Charles Lethbridge in 1961 after building the hypothesis off the work of Philosopher H. H. Price, who had also envisioned a similar concept in 1940. Lethbridge believed that ghosts were not spirits of the deceased, but were simply non-interactive recordings like a movie. In that respect, not all "ghosts" had to even be human, as it did not require the concept of a spirit or soul.

There's no scientific evidence to suggest that stone or other similar materials can store data, much less the emotional charge of energy. But, the idea itself has merit in that maybe at least some of the events being witnessed aren't ghosts in the traditional sense of the word, but just anomalous energy that just happens to be observable. The first step would certainly be proving that the activity is even taking place at all before anyone could even think to challenge or test the mechanism by which it's happening.

It's these types of activity that we want to understand. We feel that understanding something comes from observation, testing, and collection of data over time. After years investigating and talking to people about the paranormal, we finally felt that it was time to write a book on the subject. Together, with my team, we have collected and compiled our most profound experiences. We poured ourselves over all the evidence that we've collected. And while I can't promise, even a glimmer of hope of any hard-scientific proof, that the afterlife, ghosts, or demons exist, what I can offer you is a wealth of experiences and evidence that suggests that not only is it possible, but just maybe even, quite probable.

YOUR HOUSE "PROBABLY" ISN'T HAUNTED
THE BURDEN OF EVIDENCE

Imagine suddenly waking up in the middle of the night to the red glow of your bedside clock. It's 3:00 AM. The sheets are soaked in sweat, you can barely see in the thick black darkness of your room, and you swore you just heard something that brought you to this state. The only thing you can hear now is your heart pounding, the rushing blood behind your eardrums in a turbulent rhythm, and the sound of your lungs inflating and deflating as you try desperately not to breath. You're afraid to even move, but you try anyway and find that you're unable. You begin to panic, and you suddenly see the shadows in the corner begin to converge on you. You try to scream out to find that even your vocal cords are paralyzed. Your mind begins to process things slower as the adrenaline pumps through your body. You want to get up and bolt from the room, but you can't. Just before anything happens you find yourself free and scream out in horror as you sit up and turn on the light faster than you ever have before. As you look around the room, the demonic entity is gone, but the room now feels cold and deadly silent. You didn't believe in the supernatural before, but having this experience, now you do. You know you're not crazy and this was not a nightmare. You've just been attacked by evil spirits in your own home. Or, you may have just experienced a medical condition known as sleep paralysis, a condition that affects one out of every five people in the United States.

All over the world, people have experiences like this that are so profound their lives are forever changed. Some run from it, some seek paranormal investigators, and others silently suffer. Even less frequently, will you see people consult a doctor about what is going on out of fear of being labeled crazy. But, this isn't the only example. The fact is that when something strange is going on; *"Who you gonna' call?"* most people really don't know unless they're listening to the song at the time. However, was this experience truly supernatural? Maybe... and maybe not. The more important question we may need to ask ourselves is: Does it matter?

In most cases, because of the way we are wired, when people experience something out of the ordinary our minds typically write it off a coincidence or fluke. When it's something more profound, people tend to bury it. Whatever that experience really was, does it really matter if it was supernatural in nature? To most people it doesn't. We will never hear about it due to the witness being completely indifferent to a situation that really was little more than something that happened this one time. However, with others, by all accounts the experience was profound to the person experiencing it. Enough so, that they may not be able to live with the wonder and unable to find any closure until the answer is found. It's these cases in which people will finally seek the help of an outside party for answers.

As an investigator using the scientific method, I look at all paranormal cases with a very healthy dose of skepticism concerning its status as a supernatural phenomenon. However, that does not mean I'm usually skeptical about the event having happened. I find it a rare case where people have relayed personal experiences that are flat out fabrications for the sake of creating a hoax. However, I feel that many of these experiences are misinterpreted events that have actually happened with an explainable mechanic. People tell me all the time about their experiences expecting a very enthusiastic response as if I have never heard anything like it before, only to be disappointed that not only have I heard that exact story before; but I have debunked it several times. It's very hard to tell a client who is one hundred percent sure they've had a life changing paranormal experience that they just need to take better preventive care of their house. It's also even harder to explain to someone that, their personal experience (even if not paranormal) is still a very valid and important one even if there's no proof that it was paranormal. Or worse yet, debunked outright. People take from these investigations what they want to take from them.

Although most cases turn up nothing more than perfectly explainable events that have been perceived incorrectly under extreme circumstances such as stress, environmental conditions, or a hampered mental state, strange things do seem to turn up from time to time. It's a misconception, at least for my team, that we go out with equipment and have the ability to detect ghosts. Any good investigator will fully disclose that there are no devices with such an ability. If there were, hauntings would be scientific fact, not speculation. A good investigator should tell you that they are looking for evidence of paranormal activity by measuring changes in the environment using methods that can be verified. It's through these strange manipulations of the environment, temperature, sound waves, etc. that we can speculate the probability of what is going on.

Although, the probability of your location having legitimate paranormal activity is extremely low (less than a 10% chance by our findings) there are many common practices and experiments that you might be familiar with in paranormal investigation that you can do yourself cheaply, with little to no experience in the field, to assess before calling out an expert. Some are valuable as scientific evidence, some are not. But, all can provide a form of validation about the experiences that you might have had. We have tested the effectiveness of most the most common methods and even come up with many unique experiments of our own.

ELECTROMAGNETIC FREQUENCIES
(EMF)

Everyone has probably seen a ghost hunting show at this point. We all know that ghosts manipulate the electromagnetic fields in the environment, either by directly altering them or by using the energy to fuel their interactions, and that this activity can be measured with an EMF detector. But, how do we know that? Who even came up with this experiment? Search the internet for an hour and you may still not find the answer. I read an article that suggested that the entire concept was simply inspired by the 80's movie Ghostbusters and their use of the fictional "PKE" meter. While not too far from the truth, it was this lazy attempt at slamming paranormal investigators that made me dig much deeper to find the truth. It turns out that EMF fluctuation, as a connection to the paranormal, was first put forth by Hans Bender in 1967.

Hans Bender was a German lecturer on the subject of parapsychology, who was also responsible for establishing the para-psychological institute Institut für Grenzgebiete der Psychologie und Psychohygiene in Freiburg. For many years his pipe smoking, contemplative figure was synonymous with German parapsychology. He was an investigator of 'unusual human experience', e.g. poltergeists and clairvoyants. One of his most famous cases was the Rosenheim Poltergeist. It was during this investigation that Bender made a connection between paranormal activity and rapid fluctuations in electromagnetic fields. Initially, his statements about the case suggested that the connection could be made between psycho-kinetic energy and EMF fluctuations, but he would later expand that to relate to more kinds of paranormal activity after he began doing joint studies with Konstantīns Raudive.

In all the discussions that Bender participated in, it was never suggested that these fields were being purposefully manipulated for means of communication. But, rather, that it was more of a side effect of the activity that was happening. He did theorize that ambient static, and/or EMF could help energize an area giving these manifestations energy to materialize the events.

Over the years, the original theory was lost in translation.

Somehow those ideas were misinterpreted as EMF Meters were actually Ghost Detectors. Since the late seventies and early eighties, inexperienced ghost hunters have been waving the units around claiming that they have experienced activity at every spike they see on the meter. It's this inefficiency and misunderstanding of how to use the equipment that has made EMF documentation little more than a joke in legitimate paranormal studies. I challenge you to find an EMF detector on the consumer market that isn't somehow branded as a paranormal instrument for ghost hunting.

The truth is electromagnetic field research is important to paranormal investigation, but probably not in the way that you or most other investigators think. Fluctuations on a static environment are the only fluctuations that have any meaning. By holding the meter, moving around, and disturbing the molecular structure of the location, you are altering the electromagnetic waves just by moving. What you are likely detecting isn't a ghost, but more probably your own electromagnetic signature.

Detectors used for this type of experiment should be placed flat on a table with participants either as far away as the room will allow, or out of the area completely. There should be no movement in the room, and only fluctuations over a baseline average should even be considered as recordable data.

In studies which we site that EVF fluctuation were present, we note it as a change in the environment that could potentially have an impact on what is going on at the time. We use the conditions above to control the experiment as much as possible, but even then, we know we could receive meaningless reading. Electromagnetic fields are in a constant state of flux; only changes in baseline that coordinate with other events stand out as credible evidence to us.

ELECTRONIC VOICE PHENOMENON
(EVP)

Electronic voice phenomenon in theory are the voices of spirits or other worldly beings communicating through the medium of electronic devices. For a long time, this just meant recorded voices that shouldn't be there whispering in the silence. But, since has expanded to sounds coming in over static radio frequencies, word bank devices, and other such forms of communication. Typically, though, an investigator will ask a series of questions and record the silence of the room. During playback, sometimes, voices can be heard.

To some paranormal groups, EVP is the smoking gun that the spirit world is real and that it's happening in your house right now. Well, them, and at least for thirty percent of the population anyway. The origins of EVP are rather surprising and admittedly a bit fuzzy. Typically, the credit goes to parapsychologist Konstantīns Raudive. And while he certainly advanced and popularized the work in the field of EVP communication, the real credit should probably go to Nikola Tesla and Thomas Edison.

I'm not here to debate history. But, the story of these two men will forever be one of the most fascinating (and infuriating) stories of our history and the industrial revolution. I could probably bore everyone with the debate over who came up with what first. But, I have to stay on task.

Edison is credited with the invention of the phonograph. Even in his first recordings it's rumored that he would sometimes record the voices of people who were not in the room. He, himself, put forth the theory that he was capturing the voices of the deceased. It was not the intent or design of this invention, but more of a curious side effect.

Nikola Tesla, however, lived on the fringe. He had many inventions he claimed could communicate with the dead. Using his knowledge of electrical engineering, he invented and developed what is commonly known as the Tesla Spirit Radio. With the use of copper coils and an electrical charge he could pick up on frequencies and voices that he credited to be the voices of the deceased.

In neither case do many actually think that these men captured the voices of the dead. Like all new technology, it's often developed without the full understanding of the results and its potential. But, this is the literal beginning of the thought process that this might be possible. Finally, in the seventies enters Konstantīns Raudive. It's his work that would add at least a few levels of legitimacy to the claims that the paranormal could be recorded into an audio format.

Raudive conducted several experiments and demonstrations using standard magnetic reel to reel tape recorders, which were the most advanced forms of recording at the time. With the help of various electronics experts, he recorded over 100,000 audiotapes, most of which were made under what he described as "strict laboratory conditions." He collaborated at times with Hans Bender. Over 400 people were involved in his research, and all apparently heard the voices. This culminated in the 1968 publication of Unhörbares wird hörbar ("What is inaudible becomes audible") Later published in English in 1971 as "Breakthrough".

This is the research and basis that most investigators are going off of today in an attempt to reproduce those results. However, where most people go wrong is the conditions in which they are performing these experiments are not controlled. It's almost impossible to make a valid case that a collected EVP is paranormal when it was collected in a public location, there were multiple people on site, or you weren't properly tracking outside noises. There are over a hundred variables to consider before a conclusion can be made that the source was paranormal. Random radio transmissions, short wave bursts, and even long-wave can contaminate your audio. Sound waves have been known to travel for miles in the right conditions to be recorded by sensitive equipment.

While these types of recordings can be very exciting, with in advances in technology, we have discovered that many of the sounds which cause EVP can be easily identified and have reasonably explainable sources. And, although there are a select few recordings that could have some merit as evidence, because of the conditions they were recorded in, they could never be accepted as scientific proof. This includes our own recordings as well. When reviewing our own EVP's, I could put ten side-by-side and will probably flag nine of them as the investigator subconsciously talking under their breath.

So what conditions exactly make for a legitimate case for EVP? To answer that, we must first have a good understanding of how sound actually works.

Sounds are vibrations that travel through the air or another medium of matter and can be heard when they reach a person's or animal's ear. These vibration waves can also be intercepted, absorbed, and reflected by a variety of surfaces.

Sound waves, when viewed in their wave format, are measured by two factors: Amplitude, which represent the loudness or Decibels (dBA) of the sound, and wavelength, which is measured in metres (m). By using a simple formula of dividing the amplitude by the wavelength, the frequency of the sound can be calculated into a unit of measurement called Hertz, which signifies the number of oscillations per second of a wave.

$$Frequency = Hz \ (1Hz = 1 \ Wave \ per \ second)$$

$$(f = V / \lambda)$$

$$\lambda = c / f = wave \ speed \ c \ (m/s) \ / \ frequency \ f \ (Hz)$$

This is important to our research because this is the standard by which all sounds are measured. This can tell an experienced sound engineer or investigator a lot of information about those sounds, such as, origin, distance from the listener, and the acoustics of the environment.

The human ear can properly perceive sounds within the range of 20 Hz to 20 kHz, meaning sounds between that range fall within the normal spectrum of hearing. Machines, voices, and all naturally occurring everyday sounds within that range sound like the normal everyday things you are used to hearing. Sounds, which are above that scale, are called ultrasound and are probably familiar concept to most people. These sounds vibrate at such a high frequency that you cannot hear them through normal means. These sounds are produced by certain animals that use them for echolocation, and by machines that can use them in the same way in radar as well as medical equipment. Sound which falls below 20 Hz, like ultrasound, cannot be heard through normal means. These sounds are known as infrasound. Infrasound is a low frequency vibration that is produced by aquatic animals such as whales as well as a good number of industrialized machines such as wind turbines, traffic, jet engines, and generators.

Right now, there is a lot of controversy that currently surrounds infrasound. What was previously thought to have almost no effect on the human ear has been proven in recent studies to possibly cause a huge impact after all. What was found in multiple lab tests is that even though infrasound cannot be heard outright, the vibrations from the low frequency noise can still vibrate and stimulate the eardrum. In many cases this caused the human brain to detect the presence of sound even though it could not be heard by the individual. In the subjects that this was happening with, they would often find the subject would feel uneasy, paranoid, and uncomfortable. People described the sensation as a feeling of being watched. Or as if there was impending danger. Without being able to detect the source of the stimuli, the brain would tell the body that something was wrong and was alerting them of the issue by giving them a sense of dread. A separate study showed that, in some cases, infrasound was actually strong enough that it would vibrate the fluid in the eyeball, causing strange images and shadows to the subject where there were actually no visual stimuli at all.

So, while the human ear can only hear a finite range of sounds that are being produced in the world, as it turns out, the human vocal cords can produce an even more finite range of sounds. The voiced speech of a typical adult male will have a fundamental frequency from 85 to 180 Hz, and that of a typical adult female from 165 to 255 Hz. This boundary can be pushed either direction during activities such as shouting or singing. Ultimately this means, with some rare exceptions to the rule, sounds falling outside of that frequency will not be produced by a human.

This is important because often we will capture EVP's that contain what sounds like human speech outside the range of what human vocal cords are typically known to produce. Situations like this are what make for excellent evidence that electronic voice phenomenon is a real occurrence that lacks a quick easy answer.

Whenever capturing audio anomalies of this nature, we evaluate the sounds based on criteria to determine the quality and the "validity" of the evidence. We class this evidence on a grading scale of A, B, C, and F. A being the most convincing and probable as paranormal in nature, and C being the least convincing, but still possible. A class of F would denote a failing score, either debunked outright or so completely obvious that we wouldn't even consider it as being paranormal in origin. We grade each individual anomaly based on the following factors:

1. Does the sound recorded contain clear and recognizable elements and patterns of speech, including words, syllables, and a language?
2. Was the response relevant to the questions being asked?
3. Does the recorded sound fall outside the range of what human vocal cords can produce?
4. Does the recorded sound fall outside the range of human hearing?
5. Was the sound recorded in a controlled environment?

In the modern computer age it's easier than ever to record and analyze sound. There are dozens of programs and devices out there available that are suited for the task. Almost all digital recorders will record sounds in a format that can be read by your computer then analyzed visually using a waveform. This is actually the best way to find anomalies since sounds that you may not be able to hear will show up as small blips on what should be static portions of the audio. However, there are a few things that you should be aware of.

As of this writing there are two major file formats that sound is recorded in when using a digital device, WAV and MP3. Most recorders and sound files downloaded from the internet will be in an MP3 format. This is because the file type is a compressed version of the original recording and is easier to stream. This information is very important because the way that the file has been compressed is by getting rid of all sounds outside the normal range of human hearing. That means anything on the file that was below 20 Hz or above 20 kHz is completely cut from the file in processing. While this format may be good for listening to your favorite Pink Floyd album via streaming service, it's not so great for paranormal investigation. WAV files are the other most common file type and a far better suited for EVP studies. The WAV format is uncompressed raw audio and will be a bigger file size, but won't be missing valuable data that could contain an anomaly. While EVPs could be captured on a device that uses the MP3 format, be aware that they will all be within the standard range of hearing.

Just like file type. The device you use to record is important. While a phone is perfectly fine for starting out, note that most phones will record sound in an MP3 format because they are now designed with file sharing in mind. Also, the microphones on a phone are specifically designed for detecting human voice and noise cancelling. While you can get some good results with a phone, it's like using a spoon instead of an ice cream scoop to serve dessert. I have seen many paranormal investigation websites recommend cheap and poorly made recorders over more expensive ones for the fact that they get *more* results with them. As any sound engineer will tell you, this logic is horrible. The increased amount of results that they are getting are more likely due to the fact that the hardware is less able to do its job and record distinguishable sounds that can be easily debunked. I'm not sure that they realize these statements actually hurt their credibility. Rather, a digital recording device that is equipped with a high dynamic range microphone that records in the WAV format is actually the most legitimate tool for the job.

PHOTOGRAPHY AND VIDEO

A picture is worth a thousand words. You would think snapping the picture of a ghost would be the holy grail of evidence. But with the amount of software and people out there looking to stage a hoax, it's just not a reliable source of proof no matter how good the image is. I would estimate at least ninety percent of the photographs labeled as "evidence" in circulation today are either misidentified naturally occurring anomalies or outright forgeries.

Spirit photography was staple of ghost hunting and paranormal investigation since the spiritualist movement of the 1800's. The first known accounts of spirit photography, like most things related to spiritualism in that time, were very much a hoax. Spirit photography was first used by William H. Mumler in the 1860's. The technique was discovered by accident, after he saw a second person in a photograph he took of himself, which he found was actually a double exposure. Seeing there was a market for it, Mumler started working as a medium, taking people's pictures and doctoring the negatives to add lost loved ones into them. Eventually, he was proven to be a fraud when he mistakenly put identifiable living residents into some pictures. While probably not important, I'd like to point out that this is probably the first documented selfie as well.

Even though Mumler had been exposed, this did not stop many other people from duplicating the process over the years. Through the 1880's into the early 20th century spirit photography remained popular, with notable proponents such as Arthur Conan Doyle and William Crookes. Later in the game, William Stainton Moses, claimed that spirit photography operated by means of a fluid substance called ectoplasm, in which the spirits take form.

While spirit photography of the past was largely exposed for the hoax that it was, the idea did evolve over time. No longer called "spirit photography" the idea that entities could be captured onto film has stuck around. Over the years there have been numerous photographs and videos produced that seem to indicate that there is something out there. Most of the time the images and video can be debunked as objects out of focus, misinterpreted images, or outright forgeries made with Photoshop. However, there are a select few images taken which are a little harder to debunk, but with the ease of modern digital tools for photo and video alteration I would be hard pressed to be accepted as hard proof. That aside, there are some compelling photos and video out there for consideration. And when the file checks out against scanning as an unaltered file, it does raise questions.

For ourselves, we videotape and photograph everything during the investigation to create our medium to present evidence to our audience. However, there is no amount of proof we could possibly offer to prove that our videos and photographs have not been tampered with, nor can anyone else. As a means of transparency, we offer the raw files of all evidence on our website for review for any expert to challenge and test as they see fit.

Typically, in the parapsychology field, there are three major forms of visual evidence that have been circulated as the most commonly captured and accepted as "evidence".

Apparitions

Faked or real aside, typically apparitions will come in one of three flavors: full-bodied, partial bodied, and shadow figures. A full-bodied, or partial apparition, essentially looks like a person, but either appears as an entire body, a partial image, or a smoky figure all with details that make it recognizable as a person or animal. Basically, another person in the room that shouldn't be there. Shadow figures are just as they sound; They take the shape of a person, but are void of any details giving it the appearance of being a shadow which doesn't belong in the image.

Unexplained Mist

Just as straightforward as it sounds, people have been known to capture images of unexplained mists that seem to hover around areas where paranormal activity happens. Unless this sort of event coincides with an unusual activity that was happening at the time, or spikes from EMF detectors, we do not consider fog or mist to be paranormal. Many of the mists and fogs captured are little more than out of focus objects obscuring the shot, or a naturally occurring fog or mist.

Orbs

The most frustrating of all evidence is the Orb or Ghost Lights. I can't tell you the countless number of photographs I have been given to study from both private parties and professionals alike. Commonly during a paranormal event, investigators have captured what are believed to be orbs of energy in the air onto film and digital visual media. Using the assumption that paranormal entities are made up of charged energy, in these photographs they will supposedly appear as small balls of light not usually seen by the naked eye.

The problem with this is, because of the nature of light and how our vision and photography work, foreign objects in the air, such as dust particles, will reflect light in such a way that it will create the same effect as if you photographed a ball of energy. However, some investigators will claim that in very high definition videos a select few of these can be ruled out because of the behavior, trajectory, and proximity to a considering event. Often during an EVP session, at the exact moment of an EVP recording orbs will be recording moving in, out, and around the recording device, lending some levity to the claim that these phenomena might be intelligent or responsible for the activity. While it's a thought process in the right direction, it still leaves too much room for coincidence.

Monowavelength Photography™

After several arguments with other experts about the claims they made on the validity of their orb photography as evidence, we finally put it to the test ourselves. It seemed like every other group had theories, one way or the other, and made grand claims, but nobody was really doing anything to prove their case. While, I for one, personally believed that the possibility that orbs were a real phenomenon, I had no confidence that any picture I had ever seen or taken myself was substantial enough to be called evidence. Any one of them could have been dust, bugs, or any other random number of objects in the shot reflecting light. For months I experimented around with different methods of photography, trying to get a result that I felt would be conclusive enough to call one way or the other.

Finally, during an interview on a Podcast, it finally hit me. We were discussing an old wife's tale that claimed spirits were more easily seen in red light. Thinking on the matter very briefly, I suggested that if the rumor was true, then taking pictures with a red flash filter might increase the frequency in apparitions appearing in photos. Strangely enough, that was the answer to my orb problem, but for a completely different reason.

Photography and vision both work on the principle that light is reflected off of objects and the captured by the lenses of either our eye or the camera. Newton observed that color is not inherent in objects. Rather, the surface of an object reflects some colors and absorbs all the others. We perceive only the reflected colors. Thus, red is not "in" an apple. The surface of the apple is reflecting the wavelengths we see as red and absorbing all the rest. An object appears white when it reflects all wavelengths and black when it absorbs them all.

The colors that are seen are also factored by the idea that neutral or white light (containing multiple wavelengths of the color spectrum) is the primary light source. Objects then reflect the unaltered wavelength light back with the color that the object exists in.

In the case of orbs being debunked, they are almost always described as particles of dust that are reflecting light back to the camera. By using Newton's principle, if we were to narrow down the wavelength of light to a single wavelength, only that color could be reflected in an image. Thus: if we remove all external light sources from an environment and take pictures using a red light or flash as the singular light source, with a full spectrum camera, the image should return an image with only objects reflecting red light. In the case of objects that can absorb red light they will just appear washed out or negative.

This can be done with any singular color filter. Should the results include an orb of a color not on the provided spectrum, it could be concluded that such an object was creating its own light source. In that case it would be probable that the object was a form of energy.

When we put this simple experiment to the test, the results were astounding. We used three separate colors over a series of pictures in controlled environments. What we found is that, by narrowing down the bandwidth of light to a narrow margin, we were able to increase the number of orbs that were collected in a photograph. As predicted, the orbs would match the color of light being used, proving that the anomalies were reflected light. We used the primary colors as our filters on a rotating cycle so that, in an instance of capturing a light source, it would be captured if it shared the same color wavelength that we were photographing the anomaly with. Thus, for an anomaly to be considered self-illuminating, it would have to show in two of the three wavelengths of light. We tested the mechanics with a ping pong ball fitted with an LED light inside. When the light was off, the white ping pong ball (representing a dust particle) reflected to the camera as whatever color filter we used. When the LED light inside was active, the camera captured an image of a white ping pong ball because it was generating its own light source. The effect was the same even when using infrared and UV light sources.

When we used this experiment in the field of investigation, the results were very cut and dry. In the first year of using the method we were able to easily identify orbs as reflective particles as opposed to energy in over five hundred photographs.

Thinking the case was closed on orbs, we continued the experiment as part of our standard procedure well into our second and third years of investigating, still not finding any evidence that energy was being photographed as a naturally occurring phenomenon. The boasting we did during this time was legendary, and surprisingly unchallenged. However, at the beginning of 2017 we did manage to capture two images with a startling result. On one particular long-term case, a photograph of an especially active area at a location was shot using a red filter. In the negative space where there are no objects to reflect light is a green and yellow halo similar to the verbal description of a vortex. About ten feet from that area a second photograph was taken using a blue filter, while the green is washed out the same type of halo can be seen with hints of red and yellow. Knowing there were no other controlled light sources present at the time that the photos were taken, and appearing over two separate color filters, we know that these flares were in the infrared spectrum of light.

For the most part, our group does not consider orbs as a paranormal activity. However, we do catalogue the cases in which they appear during experiments and seem to react accordingly, but unless they pass the monowavelength test, they are never considered evidence by our group.

While I don't feel like any of the other investigators I have *personally* met during my tenure have outright faked evidence, it is a growing concern. Even as technology sits now, and becomes more advanced every day, it becomes easier and easier to create fake images, audio, and video. Unless you are an experienced multi-media engineer the fakes are almost impossible to spot. As a rule I trust nothing that is handed off to me that is not the original evidence. Many times I'm asked to look at "enhanced" footage or audio, which I know is sometimes important, as evidence may be hard to decipher. But, without the original, verified, file to compare it with, there is no way that I can validate anything shown to me without having to assume that it was tampered with. Sadly, in my early investigations I made the mistake of not backing up some of my original files. I would find great evidence, make some slight adjustments to audio volume or tweak the brightness a bit then save it over the old file to save space. At the time I was new and it never occurred to me that I would need to later prove the integrity of the file. There are several pieces of software and online sites that files can be used to read a file and tell you if it is original or if it has been altered. By making these adjustments my early evidence could not withstand this scrutiny, so I can now no longer present them as scientific evidence. It's a mistake I see other investigators making frequently. Nowadays, I back up all my original files onto a separate hard drive as well as in the cloud. These files are available for anyone to look at and verify side-by-side with any *enhanced* clips that I might show them.

Ultimately, transparency is the best evidence that anyone can provide on a case.

THE FIRST EXPERIENCE

Over the years, I have talked to countless other investigators and clients. I've also spoken with many people at numerous events and discussions. Inevitably, the most common question about paranormal investigation will always come up.

"Why did you get started in paranormal investigation?" After my colleagues and I share knowing glances at each other, we all usually hear some rough form the same answer that we have heard repeated so many times before.

"I didn't believe in the paranormal until... [I had a paranormal experience]." The story itself is usually unique, but the tagline is usually the same. Like a familiar movie plot, you see rehashed repeatedly. We don't dislike the question at all, in fact, most of us love recounting and telling the tale of how we first became aware that there was something more going on than what we could fully understand. It's just that most investigators can't get over the irony that almost every paranormal investigator was somehow a skeptic, or at the least indifferent, until they came face to face with something unexplainable at the time.

Typically, an investigator's first experience will be profound, attention-getting, and hard to swallow on the scale of believability. If it was a negligible experience, it probably wouldn't have been moving enough to inspire the purchase of some very expensive equipment and a time investment equal to that of a second full-time job. However, that first event will rarely be considered more than just a personal experience. Typically, it won't contain any kind of documentable evidence since most people aren't sitting at the ready with cameras, recorders, and a host of other devices ready to record every odd event that happens in their lives.

Having said that, it's not always the way. There's no formula to be followed, and not always some singular event that overshadows who they have become. Two of my own investigators have stories in complete contrast to the typical "It happened to me" story. Their reasons for getting into this field are a compilation of life events that led them down this path. The one thread of commonality being that those life events gave them glimpses into something they didn't understand at the time, and they wanted to find more answers.

In my experience, I find that people tend to have one of two responses to having an event they can't explain: Most people move on, they give it little thought and sometimes avoid it at all costs if it scares them. *Better to let sleeping dogs lie* is a phrase that comes to mind. But, then there's those of us who want to find the answers to the burning question. *Did I just experience what I think I experienced?* Typically, those people will find a big stick somewhere and let the poking commence.

I thought it fitting to start with the stories of our first encounters from before we really considered ourselves investigators. The proverbial sparks that started the flame, if you will. The stories in the next section are not cases that NTParanormal has taken on, but a rare glimpse of the profound, and different, personal experiences that started some of our team members on their path to looking for answers to the unknown.

ON THE JOB TRAINING
ASHTON ROGERS

In December of 2013, I worked for a company that was mainly involved in manufacturing retail furniture. I did analytical analysis of inventory, logistics, and some warehouse management. It was my job to build and design a new system for the company that would accurately track product that went in and out the door through different levels of production.

I can remember, very well, the feeling of being less than enthusiastic about having to work at the Lancaster warehouse for a few days. I had been in there one time before during the previous quarter for an inventory audit and it had absolutely no airflow. Today, even though it was now technically winter for the rest of the country, the temperatures were still in the low nineties. If I have one major complaint about living in Texas it's the unforgiving heat that doesn't have any care for what season it is.

Sometime towards the end of August of that same year, the company began renting a warehouse in downtown Fort Worth as a place to store some of its overstocked inventory. It was supposed to be a short-term lease, but eventually turned into an extended contract due to our sales slowing down unexpectedly. I had done a quick walkthrough in August to check out the floor space when we first moved in, but didn't give it much more thought past that at the time. Later, at the end of September, I would return with two people from the bank and a member of our Accounts Receivable department to audit a single item on the main floor after our quarterly inventory. Between the two visits, I had maybe spent forty-five minutes total in the building. Barely long enough to note that it was hot in there and I did not like it.

For the most part, the warehouse was unmanned. Other than putting slow moving overstock into it and arranging the floor, nobody had any daily duties there that required any full-time staff to be on location. Drivers would show up with a load, we would send one of our shipping guys over to unload the truck, and then lock it back up behind them. It wasn't until late November that we had anyone who would regularly even walk through the place at all, and it was mainly just to get the place unlocked and the lights turned on.

Vincent was one of our shipping guys that worked at our main shipping location down the road. He also lived the closest to the auxiliary warehouse. So, it made sense that he would be the one to stop in the morning to turn on the lights and get everything staged for the drivers to pick up product before moving on to the other warehouse. It only took about forty-five minutes out of the morning and it made things much easier for the drivers or anyone else who was being dispatched there regularly to pick up the product that had seen an increase in sales.

After about two weeks of this is when the rumors about the place finally got around to me. Apparently, Vincent did not like going to that warehouse alone first thing in the morning. He was literally unlocking the door and racing through the warehouse to get to the light switches to turn them on, and then leaving without staying to stage any orders. In fact, after about three days of having done it, he started sending one of his employees later in the day to just meet the driver at the dock to complete transactions. It really wasn't causing any issues with workflow, so nobody said much about it.

While I never talked to him personally, the big rumor was that the place was haunted. No matter what he did, there was a door in the warehouse that would always be open. He tried closing it, locking it, and putting a chair in front of it. Each time he would turn on the lights in the morning he would find the dark gaping maw of a door wide open in the back to greet him. The door was to a storage room without a light, nothing special, but unnerving to say the least. It was also mentioned that he was hearing someone moving around and talking in the warehouse when he knew he was the only one there.

However, the last straw was when he had reportedly, once again, closed the door to the back room and secured it by nailing a piece of wood over the door frame by the handle. About an hour later, after returning, while he was moving some product around in the next room, heard a loud bang from the back of the warehouse. Startled he looked for the source of the noise only to find the back door wide open and the board he had nailed over it splintered on the warehouse floor. After that, Vincent apparently refused to do anything other than unlock the door and flip on the light in the morning before sending someone else to do any loading indefinitely.

It was the last two weeks of December and my company was in full panic mode for inventory. In true fashion, there were discrepancies that no amount of asking for recounts was resolving and I was tasked with spending a few days at the new warehouse to get everything straight before the bank came out to audit our assets. In short, good help is hard to find, and it's even harder to find help that can count past ten without taking off their shoes. I had heard the rumors about the warehouse from a third party and frankly it barely even registered as a thought in my head at the time. I certainly didn't believe in ghosts and I frankly thought the stories of Vincent running through the building were just funny if not just rumors. I was mostly just miserable that I was about to have to go do a job that two people before me had failed to do and I was more worried about family plans for Christmas since I knew we weren't getting bonuses that year because of the slow sales.

That morning, I got to work about twenty minutes early with the idea that maybe I could get out of there at a decent time. After spending two or three minutes struggling with the lock on the front door, I went around back to see if I would have any better luck. Sure enough, my key finally worked, and I was inside. I had to immediately prop the door back open because the warehouse was pitch black. I forgot that since I was going to be here, Vincent took the opportunity to skip his morning ritual altogether.

The warehouse was endless in the dark and it took a minute for my eyes to adjust. I hadn't been in the building since the audit and wasn't immediately familiar with the layout anymore since they had put more product in. Also, I had never had to flip on the breaker myself. Staring into the black warehouse was a little creepy now that I was standing there, but I still didn't see what all the fuss was about. I knew from my previous visit that space was divided into three main sections by a wall and that there were empty offices up towards the front somewhere. After I was at a point that I felt I could navigate enough to find the breakers, I found myself stepping more quickly than normal. All those thoughts that had been in the back of my head were suddenly a lot more prevalent now that I was walking through pitch black open space.

I threw the switch and, after the lights finally powered on, I decided to do a quick walk around. Even with the lights on, the place had an eerie feeling to it. I realized that the lighting was still warming up and that it was not at full illumination. The whole warehouse made a loud constant buzzing sound as some of the ballasts were ungrounded, I'm sure if I had an EMF detector in that building the baseline reading would have been off the charts. Some of the empty corridors looked like prison hallways and I imagined it being akin to walking down the hall to an execution chamber. It just had a feeling to it that was confining and depressing. The warehouse seemed smaller with product in it and it didn't take me long to move through the three main floor sections where the product was at. I was immediately pissed off because I realized the workload I had been stuck with. Just as I was trying to figure out where to start, my eye was drawn to an open door in the back-warehouse space. Thinking about the story I heard, a chill ran up my spine as I imagined something peeking out of the darkness at me. I quickly decided I would start on the opposite end of the building and work my way towards the back.

Most of the morning went relatively fine. I was annoyed with the amount of sweating I was having to endure in December, but past that I was getting the job done. Typically, I don't usually take breaks other than lunch. But, it was so hot, and I was the only one in the building, so I decided that getting a drink at the local gas station wouldn't be a horrible idea. So, I put my work down for a little while to go get some air. After taking a quick trip across the street, I returned a little less miserable with an ice-cold beverage and got back to counting sections of product.

At some point while I was counting, I realized I was having problems concentrating because of a strange sound in the warehouse. At first, I thought it was a cat, maybe stuck in one of the pallets, meowing somewhere off in the distance. But, once I stopped to listen I realized that it sounded more like a small child singing a tune. I told myself I was just hearing things and that it was probably just the pitch of the ballasts humming away in the next room. Everything I had been avoiding thinking about immediately raced in my head. And after I ignored the sound as long as I could, telling myself it was anything other than the wind whistling through the dock doors or an electronic hum, I finally had to go look for it myself.

Almost the instant I decided to look for it, the sound went away. I walked a lap around the warehouse looking for the source but could not locate it. Giving up, I went back to work only to have the incident repeat itself within minutes. I repeated this process twice before I decided that maybe I really was just hearing things. Thinking myself clever, I turned on the voice recorder function of my iPhone and left it running on top of a pallet a few feet away from me. I felt like if nothing else I could at least prove myself wrong about what I was hearing. A few minutes later the sound started again, and I just stood there letting the recorder run. The minute I started moving, the strange tune would stop. I grabbed my phone and hit play not knowing what to expect.

Sure enough, I had captured the sound clear as day on my phone. I knew now that I wasn't imagining the whole thing, but I somehow had expected it to, at least, sound different on the recording. Maybe less like a tune and more revealing as to the true source somehow. I spent the next five minutes replaying the sound repeatedly to myself. I tried again to capture it several times, but to no avail, the singing never happened again after that. Almost relieved, I went back to work pretending that it wasn't anything to be concerned with.

I had been watching the clock. Other than the drink I got at the gas station, I hadn't had any breakfast. I was starting to get hungry on top of my work agitation. I was under no obligation to do so, but I for some reason wanted to wait until 12:00 PM before taking my lunch break. Some sense of dedication had found its way into my brain and I just wanted to get everything done. It was twenty minutes until I had planned to go to lunch and I already had half the front warehouse finished. I was beginning to reason to myself why it would be okay to just go ahead and take off when a loud slam from the dock area interrupted my thought process and sent me jumping nearly to the ceiling. For the last few hours, everything besides my own movements had been dead silent in the warehouse.

Reeling around, I looked towards the back to see nothing of

interest. Gaining my composure back, I quickly became agitated because I realized, very logically, a driver had shown up and slammed the front door behind him. At the time it didn't occur to me that I had never actually got the front door unlocked, an oversight that would creep over me later in the day.

Not seeing the driver anywhere, I called out like a stupid teenager in a horror movie. I was frustrated, hot, and I wasn't in the mood to deal with having to load a truck that nobody bothered to inform me about. I walked over to the front area and, not seeing the driver anywhere, began to make a round through the warehouse area to see where he had gone. As I moved into the next walled off area I could hear heavy the heavy footsteps of the driver as I walked after him. Being only 5'7" I have short legs, so this is a game I have played many times before. I called out again trying to get whoever it was in the warehouse with me to stop so that I could talk to them. I couldn't believe that they had not seen me when they first walked in.

Rounding the corner, once again, the driver had narrowly escaped me. Finally, I walked around the corner where I could see back into the main room to reveal nobody around at all. I thought this was strange but figured maybe someone was being a bit of a smart-ass. This was not out of character for some of our city drivers, so nothing really was out of place with this thought process. I figured maybe of the newer drivers were exploring the front offices where they had not been yet. I had walked by the door several times but not gone in myself, so I wasn't even sure what was up there. It only took only a minute to make my way through the offices and discover that there was nobody in the front at all. At this point, I was starting to become very annoyed since it was so close to lunchtime and now someone wanted to play games while I was already frustrated about being here in the first place.

Making the walk back down the office hallway to the main floor, I finally spotted the person I had been chasing. Just a glass door separated the offices from the first warehouse and through it, I saw an open door shut just as I had rounded the corner. While I didn't see the driver, I saw his back shoulder as the door was closing. It was a part of the warehouse I had not even explored yet, but I almost immediately remembered that there was a break room somewhere in the area. Obviously, he was exploring, or looking for a place to wait while I loaded him not realizing I had no idea what he was supposed to get.

I walked out the windowed door out onto the floor and looked at the door I just saw shut. It was nondescript and located between the men's and women's rooms which should have been my first clue that something was off. Giving little thought to what I would find on the other side, I pulled the door open and started to walk into what I thought was a break room. However, what I saw stopped me in my tracks.

It was not a break room at all. This was a storage closet, four feet wide and four feet deep, containing only a water heater, bucket on wheels, and empty space. No break room, no driver, and certainly nothing that could explain why I was standing there with my mouth agape. Suddenly very aware of what had just happened, I ran to my car to immediately take my lunch break.

I spent an entire hour at McDonald's thinking about what had happened. I quietly sipped a soda and forced food into my face trying to come to grips with what I had just experienced. I had thought briefly about going back to the main office and telling them what had happened, but ultimately decided that even if I wasn't nuts it really wouldn't matter. When I got back to the warehouse I hesitated to go back inside. What I really wanted to do was just go home and try to forget the whole thing ever happened. Ultimately it was the realization that I had left my phone, hat, and documents in the main warehouse that would force me to go back inside. I could fake the inventory if I had to, but I would need to get my stuff back to do it.

Taking a breath and walking inside, the feeling was suddenly different. To this day I can't explain why, but I wasn't scared anymore. After getting past the dread of walking back in had passed, being in the building wasn't as bad as I had imagined. Grabbing my stuff off the pallet that I had left it sitting on, I got back to work, this time playing some music over my phone to help distract me a little. Nothing else happened for the rest of the day.

As planned, I decided to take off a little early. For the most part, I had put the events out of my mind to focus on work. However, turning off my tunes and hearing only the buzzing of the light fixtures was a haunting and immediate reminder of the events of that day. For whatever reason, I decided that I would take some pictures to maybe catch a glimpse of what, I now knew, was real. I spent the next twenty minutes taking pictures with my iPhone everywhere in the warehouse. I even braved the dark back room with a flash, although I did so just hanging back at the door to peer inside. Then, I immediately slammed the door shut. After taking nearly fifty pictures, I finally gathered my stuff up and went to sit in my car's air conditioning to look through the photos.

Not really expecting to catch anything, I thumbed through all of them one by one. I zoomed in, zoomed out and was patting myself on the back for taking such good urban pieces of artwork. However, halfway through, almost by chance I zoomed in on something startling. In one image, peering back at me near one of the back exits, just feet from the black room, was the faded semi-transparent image of a weathered man in overalls. I stared at the picture from every angle trying to turn it into dust, a water spot, hair on the lens, or anything that wasn't a ghost. After thirty minutes without any luck or ideas, I resigned myself to posting the picture and sound file from earlier on my Facebook page to tell my friends about my personal experience. To no surprise, it was met with a healthy dose of skepticism and joking.

My friends know me too well. I will, and have, done things to get a rise out of people. I'm also pretty good with multi-media production. So, I wasn't really insulted when many of them thought I was playing a prank. It took a little convincing over time and showing them proof that the pictures and audio were original, untampered files. I was very serious, and I was also very intrigued. That night something stirred internally that I would have to follow through with no matter what the cost.

The next day I went back to finish my work. I still had the rest of the warehouse left to count and had already lost a bunch of time already due to this event. But, after a good night's sleep, I had shaken off the fear I experienced the day before and looked forward to experiencing something else. I arrived at the building again early and, to my surprise, I was not disappointed. As soon as I entered the building and got the lights on I was startled by repeated loud bangs. Ready for it this time, I began rolling video with my iPhone.

Recording the whole time, I looked for the source of the banging, however the closer I got to where I initially heard the noise it began to fade away. I looked all over for the source, maybe a door was swinging in a breeze? I looked around outside the building, inside, up front, and even out back. I couldn't find the source. The only other explanation I could come up with was the single warehouse next door was maybe causing it, but their facility wasn't even open yet. After checking that out I walked through the building with my camera rolling, retelling the story for my social media page. As I was doing it, the sounds of voices could be heard as I explored the building. The voices could later be heard in the video, but I was very obviously the only one there.

Knowing I had no more time to waste I finally stopped filming when the activity seemed to calm down. But, those events would replay in my mind the rest of the day and serve as a distraction that would put me behind almost an entire day. Every time after, if I had to go to the warehouse, I would do it with phone in hand ready to go. But sadly, I would never catch anything there again. Nor, would I ever be able to debunk any of the things that happened.

The evidence I collected was sloppy, uncontrolled, and amateur. But, the experiences were rich and exciting. I faced a fear I didn't even know I had and became addicted to the investigation in the process. Eventually, in February, our lease was up, and we moved out of the location. I sometimes wish that I had access just one more time, overnight, with all my current equipment and experience. But, I heard last year that it got split up between a few different companies and they had put up walls. It's not even the same space I came to know. Then again, even if I could go back, I fear that with my current knowledge all these years later I would just end up debunking my most defining experiences. I would have to remind myself that even though the experiences might prove not to be paranormal, they would still be valid. I'm not sure if I could swallow my own pill so well.

It would only be a few months later that I would begin doing regular paranormal investigations at other locations with Allie and Sara. After I had showed them what I found, they would take me to places where they would have experiences in the past, as well as, other places they knew about with rumors and stories attached to them. Our team started like any other, people coming together with a common interest. From there, we learned and gained more experience with investigating over time and developed our own theories about the paranormal. This is how I became a paranormal investigator.

A LIFE OF ADAPTATION

SARA HATFIELD

While the other members of my team have stories of events that brought them into the field of paranormal investigation, I always seemed to have an interest in the paranormal even from an early age. Zombies, vampires, and cheesy sci-fi horror movies were always my first love when it came to entertainment. Probably something I got from my grandma at an early age who used to let me rent one movie of my choice every week from the video store. But, when it came to the reality of these types of matters, it wasn't one singular occurrence that captured my attention, it was a combination of incidents and events in my life that led me down the path that put me in the place I am today. I also feel like my religious upbringing had a huge factor in the way that I perceived the world around me and shaped my initial attitude and feelings about the paranormal.

From the beginning, I was raised by parents who were very religious Christians. As in most cases, as a child, I took my cues from them. This meant, from an early age, I grew up believing that angels and demons were very real factors that could affect me on a personal and physical level. We believed that ghosts were real, however, were not just the free floating random forms hiding in the shadows waiting to pop out at the nearest passerby. But, had a deep connection to the human soul and had no randomness about it. It's hard to describe the exact nature of this belief because it was something my family didn't openly discuss with me at that age. However, my thoughts on the matter, at least during that early age, was that the "boogeyman" wasn't just real, but was looking at me out of the darkness from under my bed.

When I was nine, my parents got a divorce. This was a strange time in my life because the emotional climate had changed dramatically. Now that I was spending time with each of my parents on an individual basis, I was finding that their personal beliefs, although both biblical Christians, were different in focus. While my father seemed to be more of a traditional Baptist music minister with a sort of laid-back attitude, my mother was a charismatic evangelical Christian. This is important because growing up I was constantly faced with making decisions on what and how I believed in matters of faith. Later, I would find that I fell in between the two, making my own way and even after that would continue to grow and adapt as life events would unfold in my life all the way through adulthood. A time in which I would undergo a dramatic revaluation of everything I thought I knew.

Around the age of fourteen, while I was still experiencing things through the lens of Christianity, I moved in with my mom. As soon as I was settled in, strange things began to happen. It was the middle of nowhere Texas, so naturally I figured it was just anxiety from feeling alone and isolated from the rest of the world. It started small, a shadow in the corner of my eye, a fleeting glimpse of a figure in my bedroom. But, I never said a word. At the time I felt like I couldn't tell anyone because they might think I was crazy. We thankfully didn't spend much time in that house though, and we quickly moved due to financial issues out of our control.

The new place was fine for a while, but then it started again. Only, this time my step-dad started to take notice. Again, it was just little things here and there. Our eyes would meet when something got moved, or the TV would occasionally turn on by itself. But, it was still never spoke of aloud.

Once again, we ended up moving. But, this time under more positive circumstances. Mom got a better job at new hospital and we moved to a bigger house. The new house, though bigger and nicer, felt worse immediately. My step-dad and I didn't get along too well, and I couldn't deal with him for very long without getting into an argument. However, now sixteen years old and able to drive, I tried to be out of the house any chance that I got. I wasn't the only one who didn't feel right in the house. My cat, Frost, behaved strangely and the feeling in general there was just heavy and oppressive. There are too many events from that time to put into words, but some of the more prominent ones stick out in my mind.

Still Christian at this time, my main method of dealing with whatever it was would be prayer. Sadly though, it never seemed to work no matter how hard I tried to have faith. My cat died a few months after we moved in, which was startling since she was only two years old. Within the week I began to have a recurring nightmare. In my bed late at night I would be just lying there, maybe reading or just trying to fall asleep, and Frost would casually walk into the room. Me, not remembering that she had died, would invite her up into the bed where she would jump up and begin to snuggle. As I would reach down to pet her little head, slowly, she would turn her face towards me so that we were looking at each other. But, I would find myself screaming in terror as I stared into the rotting black pits where her eyes used to be, and the reality would immediately snap me back to consciousness, sweating and gasping for breath. As I was trying to shake off the effects of the nightmare, I would still feel the weight and see the impression of my missing kitty, then panic, pulling away the covers trying to sort out what was real and what was just a bad dream.

Later, a sleepover with a female friend went badly when she said she heard someone talking to her in the night. The experience made her feel uncomfortable and she never wanted to return to the house. Although the event was negative in outcome, it was one of the first times I felt validated in my experiences. I had started to think all the half-glimpsed shadows and odd noises were me going crazy. I started having other night terrors and I would wake up with bruises from flailing in my sleep. I also started sleepwalking again, things I hadn't experienced since I was a young child.

The hallway of that house seemed to have a life of its own and made me uneasy to no end. A boyfriend left almost in tears one night after he told me a shadow chased him down the hall. I wasn't very impressed with his masculinity, considering I had to live there. One night, after the incident, my stepfather mentioned that he had also seen something in the hall.

Immediately the electricity shut off. After I finished screaming like a baby, I went outside to see if it was an outage. Our neighbors still had light, so my step-dad went to check the breakers. A few minutes later light flooded the living room and I calmed down a bit. He came back upstairs and jokingly said:

"I think the ghosts heard us." Immediately the electricity went off for a second time. I followed him downstairs, stepping on his heels because I was so terrified. He fixed the breaker and we both went to bed deciding not to make any more comments about spirits or ghosts, silently afraid that it might have been the cause.

I never talked about it with anyone. I always had a hard time walking down that hall alone. Something about that dark corridor always creeped me out. It was a feeling that would, once again, be confirmed years later by my husband during a visit to the house when he claimed he was followed by a sinister looking shadow that followed him to the room where we were staying with our daughter. It's not often that my husband looks disturbed by anything, but he was at least two shades paler when he told me about the incident.

The day before I moved out to live on my own, I was seventeen at the time, I was backing my car out to go to school. I looked up at the kitchen window and saw something that made my blood run cold. This was the first time in my life that it wasn't just a glimpse. This was solid, and gut-wrenching. At first, I thought someone had broken in. I considered knocking on a neighbor's door and calling the cops. But, then I realized something wasn't right. Its face only came up to the bottom pane of the window, making it about the height of a toddler, but with features of an adult perfectly proportioned to the size. The face was distinctly male, but the hair was glossy and curled past its chin. The eyes though, they made me feel cold and sick to my stomach. They were almond shaped, with no pupil, just a black pit of darkness. I could feel it watching me. I could feel it hating me. Even now thinking of the way it looked at me keeps me up at night. Often, I still see that face in my dreams. The menace it exuded was palpable and lasting.

I'm ashamed to say that I left my Mom in that house alone. I went to school and afterwards I went to a friend's house. I brought him with me to collect my stuff the next day and I moved out. My mom called a few weeks later to tell me that she heard a conversation from my old room. She asked if I had come home. My reply seemed to chill her. With a shaky voice she told me she would be cleansing the house. I keep my visits short even to this day. When I'm there I make my Mom turn on the hall light before I walk to the restroom. She just laughs and calls me a baby, but better safe than sorry.

Looking back, I have no clue how I had dealt with it for so long. It's odd the things you can live with when you feel like you have no choice. It would be years later before I would have more experiences as vivid as what I was experiencing as a teenager, but they would certainly redefine how I viewed the world around me.

When I got married, and not long after, we had our first child. Needing a bigger place for our growing family, we moved into a sizeable three-bedroom apartment, which felt like quite an upgrade from our old one. After my husband switched over to full-time hours I found myself with a little bit more free time than I had before. As a hobby, I began to do a bit of ghost hunting, just because it was something I was interested in. It was easy to get started because it coincided with my previous hobby of finding and hanging out at cemeteries. Ironically, cemeteries would be some of my favorite places just to spend time due to their peaceful nature. Only, now I would be going out at night which had a much different feeling altogether. While perfectly fine going alone with nothing but a mini cassette recorder my dad had given me, I had made friends with Allie Bolton, who also shared an interest in ghosts and the paranormal. While nothing as in depth as what we do now, we were known among all our friend as *ghost hunters*.

It was during this time in our lives that Allie came to live with us, which was fine by me because it just made it easier to hang out and do our favorite hobby more often. One night, out of the blue, we got a call from a mutual friend who seemed panicked and was asking for our help. The only details we got over the phone were that they had been on a ghost hunt without us and to bring a Bible because something had gone horribly wrong. Not wasting any time, I grabbed the Bible my mom had given me years before and we both headed over to the house.

When we arrived at the house, the heaviness of everything was sobering before we could even get inside. Most of our friends were outside taking a smoke break and the looks on their faces were ones of dread. It was like walking through a hospital waiting room and seeing a family waiting for new about a family member who they didn't know would live or die. Bible in hand, we made our way to the front door. We could not have predicted what we would find. In the middle of the front room, several more of our friends were gathered around, eyes wide with fear praying and chanting. Our friend, whom we had spoken to not even 24 hours earlier, was now writhing, screaming, and behaving as if she was possessed by the devil himself as her boyfriend held her trying to calm her down.

The official story, we would later find out, was that some of our friends had decided to go on a ghost hunt. Eventually, they decided on a local spot well known for its legends, Antioch Rest Cemetery. Waiting until a few hours after dark, the small group snuck into the cemetery and started making recordings with their tape recorder. After an hour of cutting up, one of the group members decided that they would try to provoke a response by using some offensive language and taunting behavior. When nothing happened, the group piled back into the car and headed back towards the house. On the ride home, things started to happen that would cause concern with the everyone. One of the women in the group started having a noticeable change in behavior and appearance. The people that were with her at the time said she was behaving odd and started saying strange things. By the time they got back to the house the girl was having a full-blown fit, including violent behavior, vomiting, and threatening her friends with violence. For an hour her friends would try to calm the situation, but it would only escalate out of control. It got so bad that they decided to call us to try and help.

Not knowing what to do, any more than the people already there, Allie and I joined in the prayer circle that had surrounded our friend. Thinking to myself: What would my mom do? I rocked back in forth with my Bible, praying, and found myself swept into the hysteria that was spreading like a sickness and even began to lose track of time. After a while, we all realized that she had not spoken in a while. The only communication we had received for an hour had been in hateful stares and pain-filled moans. Upon realizing this, someone in the group handed her some paper and a pen asking her to communicate with us. Over the next few minutes we would receive several pages of self-deprecating automatic writing that seemed to make very little sense at the time, but would later clue me in to the state of how she was thinking. Eventually, after another hour, things finally seemed to calm down. Our friend had gradually, over time, normalized and eventually everything came to an end. Exhausted, Allie and I went home in a state of disbelief about what we had just witnessed.

It was at this point in my life I was beginning to evolve my ideas of religion and faith. The part of me still holding onto old ideas wanted to believe that what had happened was real. The other part of me that was growing away from all that was arguing that I had just let myself get caught up in a mass hysteria. Before this moment, I had trouble understanding how people could let themselves get swept into such behavior. But now, having experienced it, I knew that belief was a powerful and sometimes scary thing. Our friend, prior to the incident, had emotional problems and had been dealing with loss, something hinted at in the pages of her automatic writing session. Deep down I felt like there was probably less of a spiritual element to her possession that night and likely more of a psychological one. Looking back and knowing what I know now, I think I might have handled that situation very differently.

Regardless of my thoughts on the legitimacy of the possession, strange things immediately started happening in our home right after. Night after night we would wake up to the sounds of my son screaming in horror during the late hours. Getting up to go check on him, we would find him sitting up in bed, in a cold sweat, pointing towards his closet, wide-eyed and terrified. Our daughter, who had just started talking at a conversational level, would reveal the reason behind her growing inability to sleep at night. She complained to us that she was seeing something moving around on the floor at night that she would refer to as "demons" that were bothering her. Another night when she couldn't sleep, my husband and I again talked to her to find out why. Disturbingly enough, she told us it was because of the headless man that lived in her room who would keep her up at night by putting blood and fire on the walls. Not ever having exposed her to any kind of horror movie, or anything of the sort, we couldn't figure out where all this was coming from. While disturbing in her imagery, I still felt that it was the product of an overactive imagination. Even so, letting my maternal instinct take the wheel, I decided to let the kids sleep with us for a while just in case. After all, when I was a kid, I felt like nobody would believe me.

At one point, we let a friend stay over after a late night of hanging out and drinking. Since my kids weren't using the room anymore, we let him crash there for the night. The next morning, hungover, he would comment on having a strange dream about a headless man standing at the foot of the bed watching him sleep. Normally something I wouldn't pay much mind to, but the description sounded eerily familiar even though he had no idea about the incident with our daughter.

In addition to the horrible experiences my children were going through, I noticed disturbing oddities around the apartment that would make me second guess myself. Almost every day we would wake up to find that the entrance cover to the attic would be open at the end of the hallway. One day, when putting the cover back in place, I looked around the attic with a flashlight horrified that some creep might be living there. However, finding no evidence of this, I replaced the cover again.

The pattern continued to repeat and eventually we just left it open. We asked the apartment complex about it, but they never really did anything.

I didn't really get worried until I woke up to find my daughter standing on our back balcony all by herself. Asking her how she got out there she told us that the door was unlocked, and she wanted to go outside. Knowing that she could not unlock the door herself, I later scolded my husband for not locking it after going out there to smoke, although he swore he remembered doing it. A few days later the incident would repeat itself, only this time I knew for a fact that the door had been locked, having checked it myself right before going to bed.

Allie had several experiences of her own, but I would always find some way to apply a logical explanation to whatever was going on. I wouldn't become truly afraid until I started having my own personal experiences.

After going back to work overnights as a caregiver at a group home, I would come home and sleep during the afternoon. After working a particularly late shift I came home to crash. Allie and my son were both taking a nap in the master bedroom. Exhausted, I crawled into bed behind the two of them and quickly dozed off. I would later awake to the feeling of something pulling on my feet and dragging me out of the bed. I opened my eyes to see myself being pulled by an unseen force. I panicked immediately. I could see Allie in front of me and I tried to call out for help, but found I could neither talk nor move. About that time, I felt myself being dragged completely off the bed, I would snap awake, sweating and frantic, in my original place never having moved.

I would later find myself having similar and more frequent episodes like this that I couldn't explain. Often, I would fall asleep or almost have fallen asleep, then suddenly find that I was completely paralyzed and unable to move or speak. From the edges of my vision I could see what looked like a shadow looming over me and edging ever closer. It never moved in a natural way. The only distinguishable feature of the entity being the outline of a fedora style hat. No matter how much I tried, I would find myself trapped in my own body, struggling to sit up breaking free always at the last second. Sitting up in a sudden panic became such a common occurrence that everyone else in the house stopped noticing after a while.

Eventually, we would all move out leaving many of those horrible experiences behind us. Our kids, although in a new environment, would continue to sleep with us at night. I would continue to have episodes, however, not as frequent. We rented a decent sized three-bedroom trailer for a year. Later, my husband's childhood home would become available for us to move into when his mom decided to move out. I loved the idea of moving there because I had spent much of my young adult life living there back when we were still just dating. The two-story house had plenty of room for the family and it was somewhere we all felt safe. It was somewhere we could be permanently.

The house had some of its own ghost stories tied to it, but it was nothing I put too much stock in. My husband and his brothers all had experiences of their sheets being pulled off them in the night and my mother-in-law claimed she once saw a little girl standing in the kitchen. Having lived there years before, I knew that anything that might be there was of no threat to us. Not that I really believed any of it anyway.

We moved in and, aside from a little edginess from my kids and adjusting to a new space and sounds, almost everything seemed to calm down. The house made funny sounds, and sometimes it seemed like we could hear people walking around upstairs and voices. But nothing as scary as what we had experienced before. Sometimes for fun when visitors came over we would make up outlandish stories about things that went on in the house to see how they would react. We would later laugh as one of our friends swore she saw the lady in white that we had made up that night.

I did continue to have episodes, however by this point I had heard about an interesting condition called *sleep paralysis*. After doing a lot of research online and watching videos, I found out that it's a condition that affects anywhere from five to fifty percent of adults. The symptoms vary, but in general the part of a person's brain that controls the body while it sleeps malfunctions, causing the person to become paralyzed. During this time, they will wake up and generally have feelings and hallucinations of being held down, drug out of bed, and terrorized by a figure in the room. The condition is usually brought on by disruption in the sleep cycle which, due to several other sleeping disorders and a night shift job, I had in spades. Learning all I could about the condition and taking steps to treat it, I found I would be able to reduce the frequency of my episodes to less than a few times a year.

After learning to manage my condition better, I began to wonder how many experiences were legitimate and how many were in my own head. My past endeavors taught me that experience, however real it seems, could be altered through the lens of belief. I still had a strong belief that the paranormal could be a real thing, but my ideas about it were changing rapidly. Several life experiences had altered my religious views and I was now looking at things with a much more skeptical and educated eye. When Allie started dating a guy who also had an interest in the paranormal and a background in science, I asked him if he would be interested in doing an investigation at my house as well as my childhood home in Joshua to see if there were any logical explanations for some of my other experiences.

After an overnight investigation of my home, we found that the acoustics in the house were horrible at best. The microphones were able to pick up conversations of people talking outside and walking down the street. Because of the open nature of the house, we concluded that being alone would just give off a creepy feeling in general. We documented that because of plumbing and structure the house was prone to making all kinds of noises year-round. My mom's house turned up much of the same results. However, we would also find that, due to the poor wiring, the baseline EMF of the house would read at very high levels. After some research I found that high levels of electromagnetic fields can cause all kinds of symptoms including: depression, paranoia, hallucinations, and sleep disorders. All things I struggled with growing up.

While our findings obviously didn't explain everything, it did explain enough for me to develop an informed opinion. While I still have a healthy belief that there are things happening that can't currently be explained, I'm highly skeptical of what they are. I've shed the traditional idea of ghosts and spirits in favor of the idea that paranormal activity is just science that we don't yet understand.

I will never run away from it again.

THE GREEN HOUSE
KRISTIN MARTINDALE

When I was very young, my large family of seven moved into an old Victorian-style home in Louisiana. Built in 1903, the two-story house was painted a dark green, and we began referring to it as the Green House. Although it was repainted to beige many years later, we still call it that to this day. The man who sold it to us was a friend of my dad's, and he gave us a good deal. Only now do we realize why the house was so cheap. The day my parents decided to sign the paperwork, I overheard my dad joking with the seller. He said "So with the price of the house, there's definitely a catch, right? What is it? Ghosts? Demons?" His friend chuckled quietly and said "Something like that. If you believe in that sort of thing, I guess." They laughed, Dad signed some papers, and the house was ours. All a good joke between friends. The price was obviously low because they were well acquainted. Nothing malevolent here...

The first couple of months were normal enough. Us kids each had our own rooms, there was plenty of space in the house to run amok, and the backyard was huge and fenced in, so we could play to our heart's content. The neighborhood was quiet and there was hardly any foot or car traffic on the streets. It was peaceful, and we enjoyed it. We did, however, hear a lot of rumors about how we were living in the devil's house during that time. We also wondered why, on Halloween, we saw dozens of kids trick-or-treating in the neighborhood, but not a single person rang our doorbell. They purposely avoided it, probably because of the rumors. But, even with those oddities, the house seemed normal enough to us. Then, Mom decided that she wanted to do a little remodeling in the kitchen. A little splash of paint, removing one of the walls to make it open into the dining area... No big deal. My dad loved DIY projects and was happy to oblige. They figured, while they were at it, they'd add a back deck and open up the balcony upstairs. The house would be gorgeous afterward. So, they started the remodeling.

At first, it was small nuisances. Doors opening and closing on their own – probably a draft; the TV changing channels and volume on its own – it was an old TV; the bathtub filling itself with water – the plumbing was ancient; things went missing – there were five kids living in one house; creaking sounds throughout the night – old houses settle. It was insignificant stuff, so we didn't really think anything of it.

Then, things escalated ever so slightly. On many occasions, people would be shouting my name and I'd run to see what they wanted only to find out that no one called. It happened to all of us many times. We started pointing fingers at each other, accusing everyone else of messing with us. But one day, while my mom was home alone, she heard someone calling her name. She was confused since she was supposed to be by herself, but she considered that maybe Dad had come home for his lunch break. After a search of the driveway and house, she confirmed she was alone. Then, a breath appeared in her ear as her name was whispered beside her. She spun about, met with the emptiness of the house. She began to wonder if, perhaps, she wasn't truly alone.

Then, it was the footsteps. The house had two staircases. One large spiral staircase led from the foyer, while a narrow one led from the kitchen on the other end of the house. If you were on the back side of the house, the narrow ones were more convenient. I can recall several instances of walking up the stairs and the sound not being right, as though someone was following behind me. However, whenever I looked behind me, there was never anyone there. Things like this happened to everyone, and my mom ended up suffering the most. After one incident, we were all forbidden from using those stairs. My mother recalls feeling watched and followed every time she used the back stairs. One afternoon, us kids were outside in the yard with Dad while she did laundry. She was heading up the stairs with the basket, only going a couple steps when she heard stomping directly beside her. She froze, chalked it up to her imagination, and continued. After a few more steps, she heard stomping on the first stair, then second, then third, pounding as if something were rushing toward her. The hair on the back of her neck stood up, her heart started pounding, and she suddenly felt the need to flee. She dropped the laundry basket and sprinted toward her bedroom, panicking when the footsteps continued running toward her. She slammed the bedroom door shut and locked it, hearing the footsteps running full speed at her door. Then, suddenly, they stopped. She could see a shadow moving under the door and called out my dad's name, but didn't get a response. She was terrified, shaking as the agonizingly silent minutes passed. When she heard someone enter the kitchen downstairs, her mom instincts took over, and she left the room and hurried for the stairs. She looked down into the kitchen, where my dad stood at the sink. Feeling safer with him nearby, she took a step down the stairs. That's when she felt the coldest breeze on the back of her neck that sent chills down her spine. She felt a heavy presence and struggled to breathe. She opened her mouth to call down to my dad, but no sound came out. Then, it was as if someone had thrown all their weight on her, and she lost her balance, tumbling down to the bottom of the stairs. My dad panicked and ran to her side, and, as she lay on the floor, she noticed a dark shadow disappear around the corner of the landing. She never used those stairs again, and warned the rest of us not to. She didn't want to sound crazy, so she simply said they were too narrow and steep and worried about us falling. Dad called Mom clumsy. We avoided the stairs, nonetheless.

My parents decided to get us a dog, because every family needed a dog according to them. They went to the shelter and came back with an adult black Labrador. Dad opened the car door and led him by a leash, so we could all greet him. We met him in the front yard, all smiles and excitement over our new pet. He was very sweet – his tail wagging back and forth and his tongue licking every face it could reach. After our greeting, Dad started leading him toward the front door of the house. We followed along, chattering loudly (as kids do) and climbed the stairs of the front porch, ushering in our new family member. But, as Dad reached the door, he noticed resistance from the other end of the leash. Our new dog was frozen at the foot of the stairs, refusing to move even an inch. We all encouraged him with sweet talk and eventually got him up the stairs. But he stopped again just outside of the door. His short, black hairs began to stand up on his back and he let out a deep growl. We got a bit nervous, wondering if he wasn't as sweet as we thought he was. Then he started barking. He barked, and he barked. He wouldn't budge, and he barked. After much discussion, my parents made the decision to keep him as an outside dog and put him in the backyard with a little doghouse. We named him Barker, since it seemed fitting. If he was outside, he was sweet and playful. It was only when you tried to get him inside that he would growl and bark. He absolutely refused to take even one step into that house.

After that, things took a weirder turn. The bathroom and living room were separated by the dining area, where a large cabinet sat filled with nice china. Children weren't allowed near it for the precautionary measure of making sure it didn't fall over and squish one of us. On not one, but two occasions, my parents both heard the explosive sound of glass shattering in that dining room. Coming from opposite sides of the house, they met in the middle, worried about their kids. Both times, the china hutch sat untouched, and after searching the rest of our home, they could never figure out what made such a ruckus.

Once, all our shoes disappeared. All of them. Simply gone. My parents blamed my younger brother, saying he must have been playing with them and put them in the trash or something. They never found shoes in the house, yard, or trash. Every pair of shoes from a seven-person family just inexplicably vanished. We all had to get new shoes.

On many nights, the entire house was awakened by horrified

screaming. My second older brother, who sobbed uncontrollably, would point to his bedroom and speak of shadows that watched him from the foot of his bed. My younger brother, who was three at the time, loved to play alone in the house. He would hide behind furniture, then run out, stare ahead and giggle nervously, then hide again. He'd do this while talking to empty corners, blank walls, or the ceiling. We later wondered who or what he might have been playing with. Perhaps it was a child's imagination, or perhaps it was something we just couldn't see. My eldest brother hardly ate at the dinner table, instead glancing around anxiously and mumbling about the people who wouldn't stop staring at him. My parents were concerned for all of us, helpless as to what they could do to make their children feel safe.

When Christmas rolled around, we celebrated it wholeheartedly. Lights everywhere, a big tree covered in ornaments, one of those train sets that goes in a circle around the base of the tree, stockings, everything. One of the presents I received that year was a lifelike doll. She was the same size as me, and I liked to dress her in pretty outfits and kept her with me all the time. I had tea parties with her, conversations with her, and I pretended my best friend was alive. At night, I sat her on my toy box next to my bed and went to sleep. In the morning, I'd wake up with her in my bed. At first, I thought my mom had lovingly tucked her in with me. But my mom said she hadn't. Every night, I'd put that doll in the toy box, and every morning she'd be somewhere else: on the bed, leaning against the side of the bed, sitting on the other side of the room. I had siblings; they had to be pulling a prank on me. After all, that's what siblings do. I started putting her in the closet with the door closed. When I woke up in the morning, she was back out of the closet. So, I decided to wait and watch for the perpetrator one night. I was going to catch my sister or one of my brothers in the act. I put my doll in the closet, facing the wall, and shut the door, then climbed into bed and waited. Hours went by and I couldn't keep my eyes open any longer. I closed them for a second, then jerked awake almost immediately. My eyes shot open, meeting the soulless gaze of my doll, who was standing between the closet and my bed, in the center of the floor, on her own, staring at me. Terrified, I ran to my parent's room and slept with them that night. I begged for the doll to be thrown away the next day. I attribute my pediophobia to what happened in that house, as I've hated dolls ever since.

You know the feeling you got as a kid when you dropped something on the floor and it rolled under your bed? That feeling of impending danger from what was waiting for you under the bed? I was no exception. Anytime something went under the bed, or just on the floor at night so that I had to reach down for it, I was fearful of the boogeymen under my bed. But, I always toughed it out and retrieved whatever it was. A monster arm never reached out and grabbed me. No red eyes appeared from the darkness. I never heard growling. But once, I climbed down to retrieve something that rolled underneath. As I was on my hands and knees, reaching under the bed, I glanced up and noticed feet standing on the other side of the bed. They were facing me, pale grey skin covered in dirt and grass, nails jagged and yellow. I did the only thing I could think of and screamed for my mother. She opened the door, asking what was wrong, and I continued to stare at the disgusting pair of feet facing me. My mom knelt beside me and asked what was wrong again, but I couldn't make words come out or stop my tears as I watched those feet slowly drag themselves across the floor and out my bedroom door. When I finally emerged from under the bed, there was no sign of anyone or anything.

My two eldest siblings have a different mom from me and my other brothers. Around the beginning of the second year we lived in that house, they moved back in with their mom. The only thing they really said was "We don't want to be here anymore." So, our family of seven went down to five.

I hardly have recollection of it, but my mom told me that one morning she awoke to me screaming like a banshee. She rushed to my room, where I stood on my bed, my back pressed against the wall, my face as white as a sheet, tears streaming down my face. She asked what was wrong, but I continued to scream, cry, and stare. She noticed that, while I was looking in her direction, I wasn't looking at her. I was looking at something behind her. She couldn't see anything, and it terrified her, so she scooped me up and ran me to her bedroom. Nearly an hour passed before I finally calmed down enough and confessed that there was an old man in my room, shaking a walking cane at me and saying that he wanted to hurt me. He said that I needed to be gotten rid of; he needed to hurt me and was going to. After that, my parents let me sleep in their bedroom. Things got even worse in that second year.

Eventually, my mom, dad, younger brother, and I all slept in my parent's room. My older brother continued to sleep in his own room, trying to be brave. But that didn't last more than a week. The night he finally moved into the room with the rest of us was the night he says one of the shadow people at the foot of his bed tried to crawl under the covers with him. You might think my parents were put off by three kids sleeping in their room with them, but they didn't make an issue of it. They didn't want to admit that something was wrong in that house, but they weren't going to dispute us either.

Once, my dad woke up in the middle of the night and saw my eldest brother standing at the foot of the bed, watching us all sleep. Dad asked him if he was okay and if something happened before he remembered that he and my sister had moved back with their mom. He didn't look away from my brother's figure. Right in front of his eyes, the vision simply faded away. He has no idea who or what that was at the end of the bed. It certainly wasn't my brother, and it wasn't human.

My mom got a job as a corrections officer at a high-security prison. She worked the night shift, so she slept during the day and was gone for 10-12 hour shifts at night. My dad, who had lots of friends in town decided to use this opportunity to invite his friends over at night. I retain that he needed another adult in the house when it was dark out, but he'll never admit that. One night a small group of his friends showed up to the house to drink and hang out. One of these friends brought an Ouija board to play with. They got more and more drunk while playing with it, and one of their friends invited all the ghosts and demons out to prove themselves, laughing when nothing happened. After enough fun had been had, the party dispersed, but they accidentally left their board behind. Dad threw it away the next day. It returned. He threw it out again, into a dumpster at work, only to get home that evening and find it on the coffee table. He then took it into the backyard and set it on fire. It never came back, but now we wonder what might have been left behind when he burned it.

After that, my dad started having weird dreams, although he says they were more like visions or a trance. He felt as though he was sleepwalking and aware, but unable to control his own body. He remembers walking into a large conference room, where a man waited for him. With slicked back black hair and a nicely tailored suit, he motioned for my dad to sit in front of him. His smile and jet black, pupil-less eyes were unsettling, but my dad sat anyway. The man told him he was too happy, and he didn't like it. He said "they" needed to get in, but couldn't do it as long as his daughter was around. The man said his daughter was too much of a light, too disgusting and undesired, and that they'd have to get rid of her to let them in. Dreams are weird, but this was scary. Hearing about it frightened me even more, since I was the aforementioned daughter. Dad was clearly shaken and went through a major attitude adjustment after that. The normally happy, goofy, funny dad that played with us and had lots of friends began to act short with everyone. He'd snap at nothing. He shouted, he swore, he stopped doing the things he normally loved. It was almost like he was an entirely different person, and we were all scared of him.

In the final few months, I started experiencing more terrifying things. At night, I'd wake up to go to the bathroom and see someone standing at the other end of the hallway. I'd flip on the light for security, but it never made a difference. To this day, I recall the woman that stood at the other end of the hall. She was completely naked, dark hair covering her face. Her skin was grey and sickly looking. Her feet were covered in dirt. They looked like the ones I'd previously seen from under my bed. At first, she'd just stand there and, as terrified as I was, I could make it to the bathroom and run back to my parent's room without any other problems. But as time went on, she stopped just standing there. It got to where, every time I took a step toward the bathroom, she also moved forward. But instead of taking a step, she just sort of... dragged her toenails along the wood floors. I distinctly remember that horrible sound. I started asking someone to take me to the bathroom at night, which was embarrassing at my age, but better than dealing with that atrocity.

One evening, I was in the bathtub. I could hear the TV running in the living room, so I didn't feel isolated. I also felt like I wasn't alone in the bathroom. I bathed as quickly as I could, hoping to be in contact with another person soon, as I felt extremely uncomfortable. The feeling of dread grew, and the room felt colder and heavier all the sudden. Then, I felt weight press down on my shoulders. I was suddenly submerged in the water. I thrashed around, splashing the water and knocking shampoo bottles off on the floor while trying to pound on the wall next to the tub to get anyone's attention. Seconds passed before my mom opened the door and stepped inside to see what the ruckus was about. When she opened the door, the weight left my body and I emerged from the water, gasping for air. Mom asked what happened, and I cried and begged to leave that house.

We finally got a break later that year. My grandparents asked all of us to come over to visit for the whole weekend. We were so thrilled to be away from the house for so long. And, as soon as Dad was away from the house, he was normal again. We enjoyed our visit with our grandparents, but dreaded our inevitable return at the end of the weekend. When the time came, we hesitantly went back home. And boy, were we in for a surprise. The place was in utter chaos. Furniture was torn to pieces, things were broken, and everything was in disarray. Most of our valuables were missing, and our dog was gone. My mom called the police, and they wrote it up as a robbery, although there was no sign of forced entry, no footprints, no fingerprints, and the neighbors never saw anyone come or go from the house. We cried for Barker, since he was never to be seen again.

My parents decided enough was enough after that. After two years of terror, we vacated the house and left everything else behind. We never looked back and never returned to that place. You couldn't pay us to. Immediately after moving into another house, my dad returned to his normal self for good. He also seemed to have completely forgotten everything since that "dream" of his. He claimed he felt like he hadn't been there the entire time. We "joke" that he must have been possessed or something. Who knows what happened. The house we moved into afterward was normal, but it took us a while not to be paranoid. After experiencing what we had, we weren't sure we'd ever be the same again. Many, many years later, we were finally able to talk about what happened. According to my dad, the house had a rather large crawlspace underneath it to work on plumbing, wiring, etc. The first time he went under, he found a big, cold mound of dirt directly beneath the dining room. It could have been a well at some point, but we "joke" that it might have been a grave.

As Lead Investigator of NTPI, Ashton Rogers, says regularly: "Experiences are valid, but they aren't proof." I couldn't agree more.

Since living in the Green House, I have spent a lot of my life investigating, researching, and trying to disprove ghosts. I've watched horror movies and paranormal shows and mocked them mercilessly. I tease people when they try to scare me with scary stories. I've gone to "haunted" locations and tried to find proof of the supernatural. Years of this has made me a walking contradiction. I do not believe in ghosts and the afterlife. I do not believe in a god or the devil. But I am still terrified thinking back on those two years at that place. It may have been a fear cage. Maybe it was something in the water. Perhaps we all suffered from a 2-year case of group hysteria. I did come to learn, nearly two decades later, that there were over thirty environmental complaints within a one-mile radius of that place during the years we lived in that house. I'm curious to know if our experiences were simply symptoms caused by poor environmental factors. Or maybe they had nothing to do with anything. I don't know, and we can't know yet, but I hope one day we'll be able to understand. I'm quite anxious for the day our lead investigator can contact the current home owners and I get to return there as an investigator.

My experiences were valid, but they aren't proof. That is where my story begins.

WHAT'S THAT SOUND?
ALLIE BOLTON

I have always been a curious person. To me, learning new things was "cool" and if it had anything to do with science, crime or cartoons I was invested. I loved dinosaurs and Batman above all else, and dreamed of one day either being a paleontologist, forensic scientists, or criminal profiler for the FBI. With my deep-rooted interest in science, weird and the unknown, it's no surprise that I was also drawn to the paranormal. My friends and I have fond memories of staying up late at night to listen to Art Bell: Coast to Coast, reading Goosebumps, and watching shows like Strange but True which only help fuel my ever-growing interest in the supernatural.

Around the age of twelve, I have fond memories of visiting a favorite antique book store with my mom. This was one of the few activities that we both enjoyed doing together. At that age,

I would usually have wanted to do other things besides hang out with my mom, but going to our favorite bookstore was always a welcome activity. During one visit, buried in a pile of old dusty books, I came across a hardback with a strange picture of a pyramid on it. Within its pages, the book claimed that it could expand my mind and unlock my psychic potential. Realizing that I could have a superpower in a matter of just a few weeks, I begged my mom to buy me the book.

After I got it home, I studied the pages as if I was decoding a lost ancient text. I practiced the techniques in the book for two weeks while fantasizing about what I would do first with my new telepathic and telekinetic powers. I may have even designed a costume that would allow me to fight crime while still looking quite fashionable. Sadly though, my powers never came, and I ended up selling my secret tomb at a garage sale a year later. From then on, I focused more on science than my telepathic abilities.

It was later around the age of fourteen, while living in Everman, Texas with my mom and her boyfriend, that my friends Courtney and Natasha would unwittingly become part of my first paranormal investigation. The two of them were quirky like me and shared a love for things outside what other kids our age were into. My mom and I were living in a house that was nice, but had an off-putting feeling to it especially in the back room. I also noticed that my three cats, Scarlet, Reba, and Dude, also didn't seem to like going in there even if I was in it at the time. Often, Scarlet, would come to the door to get my attention, only to look off to a section of the room as if she saw something. Then, immediately, run away. Courtney and Natasha, who stayed over quite often, would tell me on several occasions that they would hear strange noises in the house, and had a sense of being watched. Never one to shy away from an experiment, and after years of watching paranormal investigation shows, I knew exactly what to do. With a little convincing, I talked both of my best friends into staying up late one night to hold a seance.

After dinner, the three of us sat up the rest of the night waiting for my mother and her boyfriend to go to bed, so that we could get started with our plans. Sometime, halfway through Evil Dead, the two finally disappeared for the night and we were able to begin our necromantic rituals. At first, we tried making contact in my room where we thought most of the activity was going to happen. Sitting in the dark for almost thirty minutes, we didn't contact anything at all. But, we had succeeded in unnerving ourselves enough that we didn't want to stay in there anymore. Nothing had happened, but we just couldn't help feeling like we were being watched. Thinking we might have better luck in a proper seance setting, we moved to the living room where we could all sit around the coffee table and hold hands.

Swiping some of the scented candles that my mom kept stashed in the bathroom, I set the mood. With the strong smell of Christmas cinnamon spice now pouring into the air, we sat cross-legged around our alter and joined hands. With our energy high, we opened ourselves up to the spirit world. I demanded that my friends concentrate, even though, I myself, couldn't stop giggling under my breath. Finally, after several minutes, we all began to ask questions to the darkness, asking the spirits to make their presence known by approaching the table. At least ten minutes went by with absolutely nothing happening. Just as we were about to give up, we all saw one of the candles flicker and instinctively we all held our breath.

"Did you do that... Is there something here?" I called out, and I could feel Courtney's hand perspiring in mine. This was it, I knew there was something going on with this house, I thought to myself. We listened and watched the flames intently waiting for a sign. Suddenly Natasha was tugging on my other hand, gasping for breath.

"Did... you... hear that?" she said with almost a stammer. And while initially, I didn't know what she was talking about as I looked at Courtney, we both heard it for ourselves. Quiet and distant in the background, a sound so faint and low, I wasn't even sure if we had really heard it at first. Then, we heard it again. It was like a wounded animal or a child crying. It was so quiet we couldn't tell what it was or where it had come from. I tightened my grip on my friend's hands and gulped hard before speaking.

"Who are you? Can you tell us your name?" My voice came out almost as a whisper. Immediately, there was a response. In the same tone as before, only a little louder and drawn out, we all heard it for sure this time. It was a moaning sound. Immediately we all broke contact, terrified of whatever we had just summoned from the shadows. However, it did no good. We heard the sound again, this time in the distance back towards the rooms that lied outside the reach of our Christmas scented candlelight of safety.

Straining to listen, the sound came again, and we were horrified. However, I was beginning to worry that one of the cats could be injured. Scarlet, who had sustained a head injury in prior years, was known for getting stuck in places she shouldn't be. Even though I was scared for my life, I was also concerned for my baby kitty. As a group, we all slowly crept down the hallway and into the darkness. With me holding our candle out like a torch in a Mayan temple, the other two followed behind me like the other members of the Scooby gang. As we got closer to the back we once again heard the sound, and it was most definitely, not my cat. This time it was louder. Again, this time faster.

With only a few steps between us and the last door that led to my mom's bedroom the horrific realization of what was going on crept into each of us simultaneously. In addition to the moaning, we were hearing grunting and the creaking of the bed in complaint. Terrified by the sudden visions of my mom and her boyfriend going at it, we suddenly dispersed in unison to my room. Laughing and shrieking under our breath at the same time we vowed never to venture out of the room again after my mom had gone to bed. I like to think that I learned a valuable lesson that night. But, for the life of me I cannot think what it might be.

When I turned twenty-one I made a new friend, Sara Hatfield. We shared many common interests one of which was our love for bad horror movies and the paranormal. After being friends for a while, I eventually moved in with her and her family for a while I was taking some college classes to help save money. On our free time we would drive around, and she would show me all the cool places she had discovered over the years to do ghost hunts. We would spend many weekends with an analog tape recorder sitting in graveyards seeing if we could capture the voices of the dead. In those days we did not have the same resources that we have now and our "investigations" were more relaxed. Recently, while going through some very old tapes, we discovered some of our earliest EVP sessions and listened. Call me old fashioned, but it never gets old hearing myself ask the spirits: "Do ghosts fart?"

It would still be a long time before the hobby would really turn serious. Many of our friends knew about our extracurricular activities and decided to follow suit. One unexpected incident would really sober my thoughts toward the paranormal. Once, in the middle of the night, I received a call from some panicked friends who had been on a ghost hunt in a location that both Sara and I were very familiar with. Antioch Rest Cemetery was known for its local legends and strange rumors.

The group had been out ghost hunting on their own when one of their group had become very malicious in his tactics to get a response. Mostly they were just out there messing around, but by the time they had returned to their house in Joshua things had become serious. By the time they called me, they were in a full-blown panic. After telling Sara to grab her bible, we both made the drive to see what the hell was going on.

Of the whole incident, it was the drive that sticks out most in my memory. There was just a very foreboding feeling to it, like we were driving into a huge thunderstorm and we might not make it back out. After hearing my friends voice over the phone, I feared what we would find when we got there. When we finally arrived, things had already been out of control for a long while. Our friend who seemed, from what I thought, to be suffering from nervous breakdown was in the floor scribbling furiously on a pad of paper, cursing people out, and vomiting. The things she was writing on the paper were chilling, self-deprecating, and not things I try not to think about. All our friends stood around her praying. Not knowing what else to do, Sara and I joined in as well. Several times Sara and I would go outside for a smoke break, but we could barely bring ourselves to words about what was going on inside the house. I don't know if we were scared, skeptical, or just in slow shock at everything that was going on.

Eventually, after a few hours everything seemed to calm down and everyone went their separate ways. The incident itself was talked about enough that I don't think anyone from that group ever went back to Antioch. If the incident itself wasn't unnerving enough, the months that followed felt like a living hell. Even though we had put the craziness of that night behind us, it seemed like some of it had somehow followed us home.

At first, it just seemed to start with Sara's youngest child. Almost every night the whole house would wake up to blood curdling screams from his bedroom. Upon entering the room, he would just be sitting in his bed straight up, white as his sheets, soaked with sweat and pointing at his closet door. Up to this point he had never had any problems sleeping in his room. Really, we figured it was just a coming of age, but the timing of it was something we would all look back on as more things began to happen.

Around the same time that Sara noticed that the cover to the attic crawl space was constantly opening on its own, I started to notice little things around the house myself. Most disturbingly one night an incident I can't explain to this day. Since I didn't have a room of my own, I slept on the big couch in the living room. About eight to ten feet from that was a small tower that held approximately forty or fifty DVDs. it was a typical cheap piece of furniture, not well put together, that had a habit of falling over if you looked at it wrong. The slightest accidental bump often sent the small shelf tipping over and all the contents spilling out onto the floor. On morning, after going to bed late, I woke up a little earlier than usual. Everyone else was still in bed. As I got up to go to the restroom I noticed something strange as I passed by the shelf. It had been turned completely around and was now facing the wall. The sight was a bit unsettling because I knew it had been facing the right direction when I went to bed the night before. Thinking there was probably a logical explanation for it I went about my day. When Sara and her husband woke up a little later I asked them about the shelf. Sure enough, they both said that they had not touched it. When Stephen went over to it to turn it around, all the DVD's loudly spilled to the floor as he tried to move it. Even thinking about it now still weirds me out. However as strange as that incident, the scariest moment in that apartment was yet to come.

One night, just a few weeks before moving out, Sara and Stephen had taken the kids out for a family dinner. Not really having any set plans, I decided to take a shower, get ready and go out to find some fun of my own. The only one in the apartment I jumped in the shower and took a hot shower, enjoying the freedom of not having a child knocking at the door needing to use the bathroom. After getting out, drying off and getting dressed, I proceeded to fix my hair and makeup in the bathroom. As I was doing so I heard the front door open and close followed by footsteps coming up the stairs. Out in the hall I could hear the kids doing their usual shtick of bickering back and forth while Stephen and Sara were talking. Knowing that they were home way too early to have eaten any dinner yet, I poked my head out the door to see what was going on. As I did, the apartment was filled with dead silence. I called out to Sara, but nobody answered me. I listened for several seconds and still heard nothing. Just to be sure I called Sara's cell phone and she confirmed that they were still out eating. Scared to death, I slammed the door shut and locked myself in the bathroom. Sara tried to calm me down on the phone, but I wasn't having it. I knew what I had heard. Eventually after hanging up I calmed myself down, but I didn't leave the bathroom until they came home. In the years since moving out, we've often thought back to those events and wondered if maybe someone had been sneaking into the apartment at night through the crawl space. But nothing ever came up missing, and it never explained how the DVD shelf could have moved without being spilled or me waking up.

It would be a good few years later that I would meet Ashton through a mutual friend and eventually introduce him to Sara. While he had similar interests in the paranormal as we did, they were just casual at best. However, he did have a very big love of science. Ashton went with us to Greathouse Cemetery to try to get some EVP's and while he was genuinely interested, it wasn't much more than a way to hang out and kill some time. However, once he had his experience at the Lancaster warehouse in 2013, he became fully invested in the idea of investigating and getting serious about making them full blown scientific studies.

At the time I was working a job that made it impossible for me to participate in the first "official" investigations. I had to be out of town most weekends which was when the group did most of their work. Sara and Ashton would go to locations on their own with a camera and a digital recorder to see what they could find. I would have to hear about the stories later and it made me sad that I wasn't able to go with them. During that time, I was only able to help at a few locations as my schedule permitted. One of which ended up being Antioch Rest Cemetery. About a month later I changed jobs and suddenly my schedule was free. After I was able to invest more time with the group things really picked up. Ashton obsessed with doing investigative work instead of just screwing around invested his spare money into equipment for all of us to use. Having better equipment made me more excited to really think about paranormal investigation in a serious way.

Over the years now I have participated in many cases and seen a lot of things that I can't fully explain. Although I've participated in numerous experiments and am familiar with all our equipment, my focus has been spectral photography. I've learned and developed my technique over the years and feel like I have been able to document some truly amazing things in photographs. I've seen shadows, orbs, mists, and even managed to capture some full-bodied apparitions with my camera. In a way I'm still doing exactly what I had set out to do. I'm a detective and a scientist. I collect evidence, evaluate it, and try to determine what it's all telling us. To me seeing is believing, and while the rest of the group may have their reservations about certain pieces of evidence. I have always known what is out there waiting in the shadows, now I'm just trying to document the proof. I may be catching ghosts instead of criminals, but ultimately...

I am Batman.

THE CASES OF NTPARANORMAL

It's hard to pin an actual official start date on when exactly our team transitioned into investigating cases as opposed to just *ghost hunting*. In the beginning it was just Allie, Sara and myself. Both had been ghost hunting long before I came along. I like to think that my contribution to what we were doing was organization and an avenue of legitimization. Having a science and media background, I had the tools to organize and validate the data that we were collecting.

Initially, we were just documenting our adventures into the paranormal for ourselves and sharing with our friends on social media as a hobby. However, at some point, we looked up and people were paying attention. None of us ever thought anything would come of it until one day we were asked to attend a local paranormal expo, something we didn't even know existed at the time. From there, one thing led to another and we found ourselves being invited to locations for investigations rather than having to ask.

It didn't matter what the location or the story was to me, I was genuinely ready for a new experience. After my first brush with the paranormal, I wanted to see what else I could find and document. But, moreover, I wanted to do the one thing nobody else had done. I wanted to produce evidence that was credible and undeniable. I knew to do that, I would have to go further than what the other groups were doing. I would have to use legitimate science and documentation to build a solid foundation if I was going to capture what I had seen for myself already. So, as a result, I spent as much free time as possible paying attention to what others were doing, and listening to what respected professionals were picking apart about their methods. Rather than get defensive, I looked for ways to build on those experiments, plug the holes in the logic, and learn everything I could about legitimizing our research.

What I found was that I had a long road ahead of me; a road that I'm still traveling. We're still searching for that perfect evidence produced within a perfect control. As I get further down this road, I'm finding that what I was originally setting out to do just may not be possible. However, I'm adapting, learning, and evolving all the time. As my investigations continue and we find more evidence of the paranormal, and the contrary, my theories and opinions have adapted. I still believe that there are paranormal things out there to be seen, discovered, and documented. But, I no longer have the same ideas about them that I did when I started. With every new case, what I think, know, and believe are called into question. And that's a good thing. By allowing this evolution of thinking, I'm allowing myself to learn.

Presented in this section are some of my favorite cases in the NTPI archives. Not every case here was concluded to have paranormal activity. But, each one worked in a way to shape my current perception of paranormal studies and how I perceived the things reported as paranormal activity. In some cases, we started visiting the locations before we even knew what we were doing. However, we would eventually go back with a more experienced eye to try to interpret those earlier events. These are the true accounts of those cases.

"DON'T RUN"
ANTIOCH REST CEMETERY

When I first started investigating paranormal cases, I made countless mistakes. As I found out the hard way, there isn't any formal training that a person can take to study the paranormal. There is no accredited school in the United States with a Parapsychology program, as is so famously depicted in the movies. In fact, if anyone claims to be a parapsychologist as an actual credential, you should probably run in the opposite direction. Or, at the very least, ask where they got their degree. It's a worthless piece of paper awarded to anyone willing to pay for it, and it only cost me $45.00 to get mine.

Although I made mistakes, I did learn quickly how *not* to conduct investigations. I eventually learned that, rather than try to study paranormal activity itself, what I was really striving to do was conduct a scientific study and record environmental changes happening *around* activity perceived to be paranormal. Trying to study the paranormal is a futile and fruitless effort. It's pretty much impossible to properly document something you don't understand in the first place scientifically. But, it was a while before that concept fully settled in and took root. Just like other any *legitimate* investigators, my group and I went through a ghost hunting phase of our own early in our career.

I was first introduced to Antioch by Allie Bolton and her best friend Sara Hatfield. Eventually, they would officially become my team members and best friends not long after a few more investigations. They both had experiences at the cemetery before I had come along and knew several local rumors, as well as some interesting history about the location.

Some years before I had even met Allie, the two had done some ghost hunting of their own. Many of those ghost hunts naturally took place in cemeteries and abandoned buildings. They both seemed to enjoy the hobby of trespassing on private property just as much as trying to commune with the dead. Sara, even before the ghost hunts, liked finding new cemeteries just to check them out, and one of these locations was Antioch Rest Cemetery in Johnson County just down the highway from Grandview, Texas. The little area was well hidden and secluded from the main roads, which provided a quiet spot for her to think and work on her writing projects without being interrupted.

Sara would later learn from some locals about the rumors associated with the cemetery. As it turned out, the cemetery was a popular place for local teenagers cocky enough to test their luck. Because of the small cul-de-sac across the road from the cemetery, it was a go-to place for the local kids to go make-out and smoke pot far from the watchful eyes of parents or police. However, on more than one occasion, there were detailed reports of these private sessions being interrupted by the sounds of rocks being thrown at their car from the graveyard. Those brave enough to get out of their cars to see who was throwing rocks, or braver still actually enter the cemetery, would talk about being chased away by a shadowy figure that loomed around in the darkness. In most of the stories, it was mentioned that if you were on the outside of the gate you were usually safe. For Sara, the stories were amusing since she had been in the cemetery several times at this point after dark with nobody else around. Aside from a generally creepy feeling that she would get near the more secluded parts of the cemetery, nothing had really happened to her. However, on one occasion, she did see a car pull up into the cul-de-sac only to see them speed off immediately after spotting her lurking around the shadowy graves.

As long as there have been cemeteries there have been stories of the ghosts that roam them, terrorizing all who dare enter after hours. Even then, in our early investigations, we knew not to give these stories much stock. However, it wasn't the stories of dumb kids that drew our interest to the location. But, rather, a very personal experience of the girls that really caught my attention. Two years prior, a friend of theirs decided to do a bit of amateur ghost hunting with her own group, separate from Allie and Sara. It was during that night things went very wrong. After some derogatory provocation, apparently, the woman over the course of several hours underwent what everyone would describe as a violent demonic possession or attachment. And later, with both Sara and Allie present, an impromptu exorcism. I probably wouldn't have believed the story at all if the two of them hadn't witnessed much of the scarier events first hand.

For some time after that night, Allie and Sara both, would both experience what I can only describe as aftershock events that had followed them home, such as strange voices in the house, nightmares, and furniture moving on its own. Of course, there was no real way to know how much of that was related to the events of that night and how much was a coincidence. But, in my mind, as they were telling me about these horrifying experiences, I was already drawing the connections and making my own conclusions.

The first night that I was taken to Antioch, we didn't have much in the way of equipment. We were still starting out, and for the most part, we were recording most of our evidence on our smartphones. I think fondly back those times because, even though we weren't really doing anything of value scientifically, the experience of being isolated in the dark and not knowing what I know now made for a pretty exciting time. Of course, it would be remiss not to admit that some of it could have just been the adrenaline pumping from the worry of being caught on private property after hours. With smartphones in hand Sara and I nervously approached the gate.

I remember thinking that I had been much more confident in the moments before. Initially, I thought that Sara's husband, Stephen, as well as Allie, would also be going in with us as a group. However, once we got there I learned at the last minute that they would be staying in the car across the street as the proverbial look-out. Stephen claimed to not believe in such things but also has always had a solid policy of not messing with anything he's unsure of. Allie, on the other hand, having seen what she saw a few years before, decided this would not be the place that she wanted her body found. At least not that night.

It was an overcast and almost moonless night. The air I pulled into my lungs with each breath was frigid and the cemetery was pitch black. Prior to this, I had never been in a cemetery after dark. Each headstone towered like a person watching me from shadowy distant corners waiting to reach out and grab me at any second. We started on the side farthest from where the narratives had taken place by some fresh graves. Using a pair of cheap, dollar store, flashlights we made our way through the cemetery asking questions and recording the impending silence. We used an EMF detector app on my phone and asked whatever was there to make the counter rise.

I was getting disappointed as it didn't seem like we were getting anything. I was beginning to feel more comfortable and starting to believe that the rumors and hype were little more than hearsay. But, as we made our way between headstones asking questions, I suddenly had to give pause. Though my vision was hampered by the darkness, I could have sworn I had just seen something moving in the woods behind the cemetery. I asked Sara to stop and focus in to see if she could see it as well. We both stood in silence for several seconds until she whispered back that she didn't see anything. A few more steps forward after that, and clearly, I saw something again. It was two red orbs, glowing bright and hovering at eye level. My skin began to crawl as I pointed them out to Sara again, this time much more excitedly. No sooner did she look where I was pointing did they fade from sight. To me they looked like eyes glowing red and the thought made me very uncomfortable. I don't think Sara believed me at the time.

After about an hour, Sara finally led me to the oldest part of the graveyard where the incident had happened. She recounted the story, as if I had been able to think about anything else that night, and we slowly crept our way towards the back area. It should probably be noted that Sara does not know how to hesitate when the situation might call for it. I'm not sure the mechanism in her brain that tells her a situation might be dangerous works properly. Before I knew it, she was at least twenty paces in front of me while I fiddled with one of my phone apps. Just as I was getting back to the task at hand I heard Sara suddenly stop, turn around, and call out to me.

"What was that? Did you throw something?" She said looking at me with a puzzled face. At first, I didn't know what she was talking about, but I could see her frozen still in front of me. I realized just a second later that I had heard something hit the ground like it had been thrown, but had just tuned it out as background noise. Suddenly this realization grabbed my attention and I was also unable to move for several seconds gripped by the tension of the moment. At first, Sara thought I had thrown a rock at her as a means of playing a prank, but quickly realized that wasn't possible because there weren't any rocks in the area for me to have thrown. I reasoned that maybe there had been something loose on the ground that I kicked with my shoe or somehow flicked up by stepping on it in the dark. And though that explanation really didn't sit with us, we decided it was enough to move on to the infamous location to do our EVP's.

After only five minutes of questions, we were getting antsy. We didn't hear any responses and nothing else seemed to happen. My night vision had improved a great deal and I was getting less scared of dark shadows and more worried that the county police were going to show up and bust us at any second. No sooner than we turned off our recorders did that sobering fear of the supernatural come rushing back to me.

Somewhere in the darkness, we heard it clear and defined. There was movement, close by, off to our left. Soft at first, then a little harder. *Definitely the sound of footsteps.* I strained my vision in the direction of the noise and called out like an idiot.

"Who's there?"

The sound immediately stopped, and I could not breathe. I could see clearly, despite the darkness, and there was nothing there. Suddenly Sara's grip on my arm tightened to an unbearable level as we heard the sound again, this time from the darkness somewhere to our right. The sound was closing in from different directions. As all this was happening, I realized that I was moving toward the gate at a very fast pace, Sara in tow.

"Don't run," said Sara in an agitated, but surprisingly calm, tone as if she had pulled the thought right out of my head. Leaving the cemetery as fast as possible, I dared not look back, scared of what I might see staring back at me.

It wasn't until we were at least a mile from the spot that Sara finally started talking again. Up until that moment, we had all been joking around trying to shake off the strange feeling we had about the whole situation. When we stopped at a gas station for a bathroom break, that's when Sara told me that she had seen something while we were leaving. Near one of the clusters of old graves, a part fenced in, she saw what looked like the shadow of a person standing there watching us menacingly as we pretended not to run from the location. I didn't see it myself, but I knew exactly what she meant. I had felt it watching us the whole time.

There was nothing in our pictures and nothing in our audio to validate our experiences, except the sounds of fear in our voices. It didn't matter, we knew what had happened. We even started to de-rationalize the rock incident in our conversations about the investigation. I knew it would only be a matter of time before I would go back, and I used my downtime to prepare.

Within a month I had saved back and purchased a camera online that could film in the dark, as well as, a cheap digital recorder and an EMF detector. While I waited for my camera to arrive at my doorstep, I did some internet research on the location. It wasn't hard to find message boards containing the rumors that had been relayed to me. But, I wanted to know more. Was there any truth behind those urban legends?

After spending weeks surfing message boards, I was never able to actually get anyone to message me back any details about what they had posted. In some cases, those posts were a few years old and I doubt any of them were even checking those threads at that point. Considering the claims to all be red herrings, I decided to focus my energy on doing historical research of the area. I knew that the cemetery, itself, had a Texas historical plaque posted out front, so there had to be information to be found.

Looking into the historical records online, I was able to find out that Antioch was originally a community that was located about four or five miles north of Grandview. The town of Antioch was founded in 1850 by J.F. Spurlock, who opened a general store in the area. From there other people settled in and eventually built a school in the center of town which would also serve as a church and town hall. However, as the railroad came through, only two miles from Grandview, the town was faced with a slow economic decline.

It was this shift that made the businesses relocate to Grandview and, eventually, the school became the new town center on the land that is now the Antioch Rest Cemetery. In 1855, the school that was remodeled and expanded onto land that was given by William Hurley for also functioning as a Methodist church, burned down. Because there was contention between the Baptist and Methodists, who had both been using the building, the Baptist group built west of the cemetery on what is now the Walter Basham place, who has family history dating all the way back to before the fire. The Methodists went further south to land, which now belongs to Raymond McElroy, and called their church/school Hamilton's Chapel in honor of the Methodist preacher, Dr. Sam Hamilton.

Rumors have persisted over the years that the fire was not accidental. The Methodists and the Baptists had their differences and there was suspicion that arson on one side or the other was involved. Another rumor suggests that the two sides might have colluded to burn the building down to split the insurance money so that they could go their separate ways in a town that was drying up economically. No matter what the case, I could not find any evidence to suggest that anyone had been injured or died on the property.

In all the pages of records, I did find one story of a woman known only as "Annie" who died June 1st, 1867 near Grandview Texas. The only information available was that she and her boyfriend entered the town of Grandview the night before. It was thought that they were passing through on their way out of

Antioch. They were seen at several locations in Grandview getting ready for their trip. The next day her body was found in an alleyway cut up. Nobody knew who she or the man was. However, the name "Annie" was embroidered on a handkerchief found near the body. Nobody was able to find a next of kin in either Grandview or Antioch, and Annie was buried in an unmarked grave in the Grandview cemetery. For years after, people reported seeing the apparition of Annie in many different places between Grandview and Antioch. It was speculated that her spirit wasn't at rest because the grave had not been marked. Eventually, though, the city put together funds to have a headstone placed over the plot.

About a month later, my equipment finally arrived, and we wanted to go back. Allie was working weekends at the time, so Sara and I decided we would go on our own. The car ride suddenly became tense as we got about a mile from the cemetery. It was like we knew we might be driving to our impending doom. Things got quiet as a slowly pulled into the spot across from the cemetery. We sat there several minutes peering into the darkness from the car before getting out. The trip almost ended right then and there when we suddenly heard a loud *thunk* against the car. It sounded like someone had just thrown a rock. Neither one of us screamed when it happened, but neither one of us were making any kind of movement either.

Finally, Sara broke the silence as she opened her car door to get things rolling. I physically had to shake off the effects of my fear. We got out the new camera, turned it on, and I started recording. Sara oversaw the digital recorder and started rolling as well.

The moon was out tonight, it was a little brighter. I could see all the way to the back fence and wooded area this time. The place seemed a little smaller than what I remembered the first time. I quickly scanned for trespassers and ominous shadows. Nothing. We opened the gate and went inside, retracing our steps from the first night we were there. We spent a lot more time to do our EVP's this time. For some reason, I thought that having the camera there would make things less scary since I would be able to see in the dark. What I found was the exact opposite. After even just a few minutes of staring at the glowing screen on the camera, I would get blinded. Looking away into the darkness would instantly cause ghosted images burned into my eyes to appear on the pitch blackness. I jumped several times thinking that I could see a face near me in the darkness, but it was just my own stupidity.

While we were together we found that not much was happening. Rolling back on the recorder, we were not getting any kind of responses that we could really convince ourselves were anything more than random noises caused by nature. After a few hours of sitting in the darkness, we caught only one piece of evidence that even ourselves didn't think much of. Near one of the Masonic graves located in the old part of the cemetery, near where we heard footsteps before, we caught what we would eventually decide was an energy orb.

Frustrated at the lack of activity after having been so scared the first night, we started to talk about wrapping up. To wrap up the investigation we headed over to the section where Sara had seen a person standing on the previous trip. I immediately gave pause as my EMF meter began to rise.

As we got near the area, I realized that the spike was getting stronger. I double checked to make sure it wasn't my own movement that was triggering the instrument and sure enough, I was getting a steady reading. We called out to the darkness for whatever to manipulate the reading. And, while we couldn't seem to get an intelligent response to coordinate with our requests, the reading was not going away but seemed to fluctuate even while I wasn't moving.

As we stood there by the rusted gate, we both heard the chilling sound of laughter from the darkness. We had been live-streaming to our YouTube page the whole time, and even the comments seemed to light up as the few viewers we had at the time had heard the sounds over the live-stream. We strained to hear in the darkness and we did, in fact, hear it again. Light and playful, like a child. Almost as the realization that we heard child's laughter hit us did I notice that Sara had been standing on a child's grave. As I pointed it out, our blood froze. Here we were standing in complete darkness in a spot where Sara had seen something terrifying, our EMF meter had just got readings, and now we were hearing this laughter with our own ears.

Sucking back my fear I leaned into the darkness, afraid to take any steps forward in fear that something would reach out and grab me.

"Hey, who are you? We don't want to hurt you... Do you want to come play with us?" I said to nothing as Sara cringed at the horrible question. We both fell silent peering into the blackness, waiting for anything to happen.

Suddenly without warning, a shriek pierced the air somewhere in the black. Our heart jumped up into our throats and we lost the ability to move. Something had just audibly cried out, loudly. It sounded like death and neither of us could react. The live-stream lit up again as everyone heard what happened. I was almost in tears as I laughed and cried through my fear. It was an odd mixture of emotions. Sara had checked out momentarily, but was starting to come back around as she reassured me verbally that everything was going to be okay.

What we heard was the sound of a predator catching its prey. A small rabbit or fox, maybe, snatched up by a large owl screaming in the distance. The sound caught us off guard and flooded our body with adrenaline. After we regained the ability to think, we realized that the incidents were unrelated. With just a little more experimentation we were able to figure out that the strange EMF readings were coming off the iron gate that enclosed the small cluster of graves. We also concluded that the shadowy man that Sara may have seen could have just been a tall strangely shaped grave inside the enclosure. At that, we wrapped up for the night and we knew it wouldn't get any better than that.

It would be several months later, after having done investigations at a few other places, the subject of Antioch came up in conversation. My sister, Kady, had been attending some of our investigations with us and was curious about the location after we described our experiences to her. Not having anything better to do, and having even more equipment by this time, we decided to make yet another trip out to the cemetery to try to stir up some activity. It had been a little while since I had been to the location, and I had already learned a lot about investigating by this time. Having similar experiences at other locations that I was able to debunk with some basic logic, I was curious to go back and see if I had the same outlook on Antioch that I did before.

We pulled up to the gate about an hour after sunset and peered inside. Nobody around to bother us and no sight of any headless boogie men to chase us out. I pulled the car into the usual spot and, once again, we waited for a minute. Sure enough, we were greeted by an all too familiar sound... *Thunk*. On cue, my sister jumped, but this time I had my wits about me. I opened the door and immediately got out looking around. Using a flashlight, I checked the ground for rocks. As I was doing so I heard the sound even louder as something cracked hard off the roof of my car. It was at that moment my suspicion was confirmed. The hood of my car was facing away from the cemetery. If anything had been thrown from that direction it would have hit the back of my car. Looking at the ground I noticed large acorn like nuts laying around all over the place. I waited a little longer and, sure enough, as soon as the wind picked up two more objects glanced off the roof of my car, only this time I had been watching.

What none of the rumors on the internet mention about parking across from the cemetery is that the cul-de-sac sits under a gigantic pecan tree. I had never given it much thought before because I was always so amped up to go into the cemetery. The sound of rocks hitting the car was not rocks at all, but rather, pecans falling out of the ancient tree onto our vehicle.

We headed to the cemetery. This time we were armed with a camera, a better-infrared light, a digital recorder, and an actual EMF detector. Having a new person with us, we began to recount the story of what happened the first time we were there. As we stood in the middle of the cemetery, I caught sight of the glowing red orbs in the woods again. Just as fast as I called it out, Sara and my sister took off towards it and I struggled to follow them with the camera. As we all got closer the lights once again faded, but not before Sara was able to confirm she had seen them as well this time. We combed the darkness with our flashlights to no avail.

After running some standard EVP sessions together, we decided to split up. This was a tactic we had started using at other locations that seemed to have a little success and we were curious to see what might happen this time. With the girls on one end of the graveyard and myself on another, while out of immediate earshot, we each began to try to elicit responses with our respective devices.

The isolation of being separated was deafening. I may as well have been on another planet. Looking back at the footage I can hear the hesitation in my voice as I ask whatever is there to interact with me. Eventually, it seemed we would be able to get a response. After talking to the darkness for what seemed like forever we heard three knocks in response. Looking up, I could see Sara and Kady were also reacting to the noise. As we all scrambled towards the source we eventually met up in the center of the cemetery.

As we discussed possible sources for the noise, I began to feel a strange sensation crawling up my spine. It wasn't uncommon for me to get creeped out when things were going on, but I asked Kady to point the EMF detector at my back just in case there was something to document. For the next few seconds, she would read off numbers as they climbed then eventually dropped off. The whole time I struggled to keep my composure. I was a combination of excited and scared. Only minutes after that interaction we would capture some very weak EVP's that seemed to be the responses to question, but the audio wasn't clear enough to really discern what was being said.

All in all, it was an exciting night, but after the investigation, my team pulled together to do some real research. Later that week, I would go back with Allie to do some poking around during the day to take some stock footage for the video I was planning to make. It was this trip that I really began to understand the mechanics that were fueling the haunting that was plaguing the cemetery.

Pulling up during the day for the first time was a surreal experience. This place I had been to many times before was literally being seen by me in a whole new light. Pulling up to our spot, I could see the scope of the giant pecan tree and it was so painfully obvious that I immediately felt embarrassed for ever having felt uneasy about the sounds in the first place.

We walked the perimeter and found that the train tracks that we had known were somewhere nearby actually cut only about ten feet from the fence line due east of the property. Even in the daytime we realized that, as we were talking, that the elevation of the tracks that we couldn't see during the night time was reverberating our voices back to us. There was hardly anything that could be said in certain parts of the cemetery that didn't echo off the tracks and the rocks that lined the creek on the back wall of the cemetery. The effect was amazing, but hardly paranormal when staring at it during the daytime hours.

We looked for animal dens, but eventually couldn't find any. However, we did note several places where we could see animal tracks in the dirt. It was likely that smaller animals made their homes in the creek bed behind the property on the other side of the rickety barbed wire fence. We reasoned that the footsteps that Sara and I heard the first night were likely animals running around in the dark. We also took note of the strange sounds that the fence made when the wind caught it, something that would have made us wet our pants in the pitch blackness.

As we were taking pictures of the older areas of the cemetery, having come to the realization about the car, I began to look at things from a new angle. I retraced the steps that Sara had taken the first night when we heard the object gets thrown and looked at the relative location. Sure enough, there were trees overhead. I'm not a botanist by any stretch of the word, but it was a pretty easy guess that something fell out of the tree that night. Also, while in that area, I noticed something about the older freemason headstones. In the daylight, they seemed to shimmer. It dawned on me finally that the material these were made from caused a strange reflective light. Passing cars, flashlights, and even IR cameras. This was a solid explanation for the orbs I was constantly recording in this part of the cemetery.

It was humbling, to say the least, to see the location in the daytime and realize just how close the property was to residential land. Just on the other side of the creek were two houses that, during the day, could be seen through the trees. Ironically, we could hear the conversations that two people on their back porch were having as clear as day as their dog paced up and down the fence line watching us. We had absolutely no idea how close we had been to people's houses and I wondered to myself if these people had been messing with us on those nights. As I thought on the topic for a minute and stared at their property, I saw another man walk out of his back door. Allie was kind enough to point out the red security light sensor that blinked on and faded near their porch light.

Eventually, we wrapped up our day trip and I came away with an entirely new perspective on the experiences we had there. Finding that the experiences I had weren't paranormal at all didn't make them any less valid. Quite the opposite. Putting context to the events of our investigation helped me to gain valuable insight to understanding how people could come to think events are paranormal, even if from the outside they obviously are not. Not seeing the forest through the trees may seem obvious to someone standing outside it. But when you experience it for yourself it's a different story altogether. Eventually, we went back and made another video pointing out all the interesting things we had learned. Filming the video that night brought a sense of closure that, before that point, I had not had during an investigation. I wouldn't have guessed that night just how far I was willing would to go recapture that feeling.

BORED TO DEATH
THE CARTERSVILLE GHOST TOWN

Leaning forward in my chair and focusing intently on the computer screen, I couldn't believe what I was seeing and hearing. Once again, after several hours of investigating without any real notable incidents, here I was finding clip after clip of evidence in our recordings. Sure, little things had happened that we took note of, but we were pretty sure that we would just end up debunking them later when watching the footage. It was mind boggling to me how the most boring place in Texas could be so active and none of us the wiser while it was going on around us. And, through dumb blind luck I just happened to have the camera pointed at the right place at the right time.

Cartersville (or Carter as it's known today) has a rich history and even more rumors of paranormal activity that surround it. Countless amateur groups have shot videos out there making all kinds of wild claims about the amount of activity they experienced. Rumors that the piano will play itself, or that on quiet nights you can hear a Comanche raid are just a few of the things you will find with a simple internet search.

We were first introduced to Carter by my sister, who had found the forgotten relic languishing away on the cusp of Weatherford and Springtown. She and her husband had done some investigation work there prior to NTPI with another group, and swore by the amount of activity they had received. At the time she didn't know that it was a popular local spot for armature paranormal investigators to do EVP's. It's amazing that we never ran into any other groups while we were out there.

These days not much is left standing of the original structures that we were fortunate enough to investigate. Originally, at the time we were doing our work, there was still an old church with a pavilion area that we were able to explore, surrounded by several historical markers detailing out the very significant history of the area. At the time we were running our investigations, the building was still wide open to the public. But, over time as more people showed up to check out the building, the owners of the property would board up the old church over and over to keep people out. But, trespassers would just tear the boards down to get in anyway. At one point, just a month before our final investigation, a group of people had broken in, spray painted a pentagram on the floor of the church and killed an animal. Years of vandalism, trespassing, and age made the structure so unsafe that the landowners eventually had to tear everything down completely.

Pulling up at Carter for the first time was surreal, it was like a piece of history perfectly preserved for us to experience ourselves. It was a hot night in January and there was no airflow through the area at all. It should have been cold, but this is Texas we're talking about. As we walked the grounds we read the markers out loud, piecing together the story of the past that Carter had to tell us.

I really feel like with enough time that any place can be forgotten and eventually buried no matter how significant it was. Long after we're dead and gone, the relevance of the past just seems to fade away after a while and nobody seems to really remember or care. It never ceases to amaze me how much of our history just gets lost because it seems like nobody is paying attention. It hurts me, because it's that past and lost connection that really makes me understand the world around me. I feel like history takes a backseat to the relevancy of our daily lives, which is sad because there are so much interesting, wondrous, and critical things that we could learn from our history if we just look at it objectively.

The main marker, which sat in front of the fragile and faded white church, told us the official story of the town that no longer stood there. "Cartersville was founded in 1866 by Judge W. F. Carter, Henry C. Vardy, and Thomas Parkinson, Cartersville was a thriving community for many years. At its height, the town boasted two main thoroughfares, Main Street and College Avenue. Local businesses included stores, a blacksmith shop, corn mill, flour mill, and cotton gin. A post office opened in 1867, and the town also included homes, a school, and two churches. The name of the town was changed to Carter in 1888. By the early 1900s the town began to decline, and little now remains of the community."

We felt like the marker was a bit of an understatement. From what we could tell, since its decline there was no community left to be mentioned. Later, according to our research, we would find that Carter had been basically abandoned for a little more than 70 years after the old flour mill was burned down. What this marker was missing was the story within the story. When the old flour mill burned down, it claimed the lives of six workers. It was really the last bit of tragedy that the town could stand, and it saw a full out economic collapse. Carter was absorbed into Springtown and ultimately forgotten about for years when the land got divided up into farms. But, as bad as that was, it seemed like Carter was doomed from the start.

Years before the fire, Carter saw its fair share of tragedy. On the very site where we were investigating another marker, hidden in brush, told us that in 1873 a cattlemen's dispute was abruptly settled when, during a gunfight, a homeowner on a land lease, was shot down on his front steps and left to die in his front yard. A friend who had been present at the time was wounded and rode away unassisted. The name of the homeowner was lost over time. But, it was known that the friend eventually came back and buried him on the property in an unmarked grave.

Some of the last skirmishes between white men and the Comanche nation occurred here. Another harder to spot marker lists the names of "Seven Rugged Riders." These seven men are credited with trying to recapture a little girl that was taken from the area by the Comanche. However, as our research would later turn up; The men would ride north to take out the Comanche camp, but the little girl would never be found. Some theories suggested that the little girl never existed and was simply an excuse to fight the Comanche and expand territory. Although, many accounts would claim that they had captured the little girl's voice on audio recordings.

The landscape of the location was creepy unto itself. The whole place was bathed in the glow of a single street lamp that was placed out a few yards from the church. It wasn't enough light so that you could even see what you were doing. But, enough so, that you could feel the presence of the building watching you at night. Most of the area was covered in dark contrasting shadow and really made every corner unnerving to gaze into. The location consisted of a one room church building, cracked and weathered with age. There was no longer any glass or a front door that was attached to the abandoned building, so the inside just looked like a dark uninviting pit to get lost in.

A few yards away from the old white church was a pavilion area covered with a wooden canopy. The pavilion may not have been original, but it looked well-aged. The whole thing sat on a roughly smoothed out surface of rocks and rubble, which was sparsely populated with ancient wood benches in no discernable configuration. Sitting at the front of the pavilion in a small wooden enclosure was a piano that looked like it had been sitting there since the 1800s. As anyone would do, I placed a finger across a couple of keys and attempted to play a note, but no sounds would come from it.

After a short walk around, we began to get out our equipment. On our first night there we started off very simply. Just an audio recorder and a digital camera to see if there was anything there worth coming back with more equipment for. We started by going in the church. Just walking towards it unnerved me to no end. As I approached the front door, the hairs on the back of my neck stood on end. Something inside me was telling me not to go into the building. But, I did anyway. Looking like a coward in front of my friends is one thing, but my sister was there with me, so I had to suck it up.

Ironically, once inside and my eyes adjusted to the darkness, I was overtaken by an immediate sense of calm. I no longer felt exposed as I did outside. The building was quiet and still. Any apprehension I had felt about the place coming in had immediately melted away. In fact, I didn't even feel like we would encounter any activity now that the adrenaline rush was behind me.

To no surprise, after about an hour of EVP's and pictures inside the building, we had no experiences and we were pretty sure we hadn't caught anything on the recorder either. So, we moved outside to the pavilion area to see if there was anything that lurked out in the open. To this day I don't know why, but when I left the building, once again I felt uneasy. Being inside it felt safe, but any time I would be outside the building I felt like there was something inside glaring out at me from the darkness. In the hour we investigated the pavilion area, I would constantly look over my shoulder, several times, back towards the church and take pictures. I never did shake the feeling, and sure enough, I would later find what looked like a face staring back at me in one of the images out of the side window. An image that still disturbs me when I look at it. I have no evidence that the face was paranormal, in fact, it could very likely just be a shadow. But, the way I was feeling at the time gives it a place in my mind as fitting what I expected to see there.

Unlike our experiences inside the church, our time in the pavilion proved to be fruitful. At one point I asked for the entities to lead us in hymn and asked them to play the piano, about a minute later we would hear what sounded like faint piano notes that we would reason was the wind blowing across whatever strings were left in the instrument. Later I would ask if "they" liked us being there, to which, Sara would hear a very faint "No" that would be captured on our recorder. Finally, after reciting some names from some of the many plaques that lined the area, we asked the entities to let us know if they were there when we called out their name. When Sara mentioned the name William Curry (one of the seven men who rode against the Comanche) a loud bang could be heard somewhere nearby, but we never could locate the source.

Despite the little bit of evidence that we thought we might have captured, we were growing bored. Typically, on an investigation, nothing paranormal will happen. But, usually there will be something going on that we can at least spend our time debunking, but not in this case. Other than the few things we heard, there was just really nothing exciting happening at all. It is a problem that would crop up several times at Carter and other locations later.

It wouldn't be until later in the week before I had a chance to really go over our tapes. Considering our experiences, it just wasn't very high on my priority list. However, had I known what I would find, I may have been a little more expedient.

Over the course of the night we would discover that we had captured several EVP's that we previously had no idea that we caught. Even though we did a live playback, many of the anomalies were so quiet we just couldn't hear them without headphones. It also helps that, when analyzing audio on the computer, I'm able to view the waveform and see the sounds on my screen. As I would highlight each of these and boost the volume, I would find that whatever was at Carter was much more talkative that we had previously anticipated.

The most troubling of all the evidence that we recorded that first night was the faint sound of a young female voice responding to Sara's question of "Do you need anything?" with the single word "Help." This EVP would appear on our audio file while I would snap the picture of a skull-like face in the empty black space of the church window behind me. It was only after showing all this evidence to Sara and Allie did they agree that we should go back with more equipment to try to find an explanation for the things we had captured.

Our group returned to Carter in May 2015 and the investigation would unfold in much the same way. We always look back on Carter as a valuable lesson in serious investigation and one we always try to warn our clients about in residential cases. Paranormal investigation, for the most part, is boring. Most quickly learn that it's nothing like what they have seen on television. There are very rarely jump scares, disembodied sounds that you hear at the time, or moving objects to be captured. For the most part, it's a couple of people sitting in a room talking to a tape recorder telling each other to stop making sounds. It's a lot of silence, followed by more silence and sitting very still. The more people you add on top of that, the more boring the situation becomes and the harder it is to control the environment. I found out that lead investigators spend an inordinate amount of time shushing background chatter from bored investigators and clients.

This time our group consisted of two new people, my now full-time photographer, Allie Bolton, and Justin Barton, who would soon become my brother-in-law. Normally Justin would not come with us on investigations, but my sister had pressured him into this one. I would find when we got there that he was terrified of the building, as he had had an experience inside. I can still hear him telling all of us that there was no way he was going back in there as my sister pushed him through the door.

For the second investigation I took our video camera with us, a few EMF detectors, and a geophone that would respond to vibrations. One by one we all piled into the church. Once again, I gave pause before entering. Something about this building just didn't feel right to me. Even with my friends inside looking in, I felt a sense of dread and uncertainty that I had to shove way down into my stomach just to continue. I've never claimed to have any kind of sensitivity to paranormal things, but there was just something about this location which always gave me a bad feeling about the place.

After finally getting myself inside and all of us taking our positions, we began our investigation. After about ten minutes we would realize that even though we had hit record on both the camera and the digital recorder, nether were doing what they were supposed to be doing. Sara's recorder had turned itself off completely after the batteries died, and the rechargeable battery on my video camera would also go completely dead even though it had been at full charge earlier in the day. I hate assuming that anything paranormal is happening when equipment malfunctions. At the time I would guess that maybe I just had taken that particular battery off the charger too soon and switch it out for another. But, this would not be the first time this problem has happened to us on investigations since then. Thinking back on, I give the incident more stock now than I did at the time.

After getting everything up and running again, we started from scratch. We started again by letting my sister take some baseline EMF readings in the church. While she was doing this, through the viewscreen of my camera, I noticed a growing tension with Justin who chose to sit near the exit. Likely this was to make a quick escape if needed. As Kady took measurements and called out numbers to the group, I began to wonder about the experience Justin had that had made him so scared of this place. I hadn't yet asked because I didn't want his story to affect my experience in any way. But, I found myself growing more curious. As I wondered to myself and watched Justin sit in silent agony, in my camera I suddenly noticed an orb shoot straight up out of Justin just as my sister was calling out a reading on the EMF detector.

Normally I'm not one to put any stock in orbs, but I noticed two things when it appeared. For one, my sister had just noted a 1.5 mG spike on her meter while she was sitting still. Also, Justin seemed to react to it by re-adjusting in his seat and looking directly at me as if to let me know he had just felt something strange happen. His eyes looked startling in the viewfinders night vision as I called out the anomaly. He did not look pleased about the information. I was afraid for a moment that he might get up and leave, but he very visibly restrained himself.

As we moved on with the investigation, Sara began by asking questions while we all sat in silence. I continued to film Justin, I just had a feeling that somehow all his tension was going to give us what we needed. It wasn't even a full minute later another orb shot directly up from his body and disappeared within the same frame. Once again, he looked right at me then asked the room if anyone had any some Ibuprofen. Kady asked him why and he admitted that he had just suddenly had started to have a headache come on. Not wanting to risk any more agitation, I did not mention the second orb. I began to wonder if this place was having a legitimate negative effect on him, or if it was just his own apprehension about the place that was causing his stress.

We tried several experiments inside the church. We left the recorder running while we asked the spirits to make their presence known by either talking or tapping on the geophone. No matter what we asked, it seemed for a long time nothing would happen, and we were beginning to grow restless, yet increasingly paranoid as it felt like something was watching us the whole time. I know that several times I would check over my shoulder expecting to see someone standing off in the corner. While I didn't notice at the time, later I would find that at one point I managed to pan the camera past the front door. In the darkness the shadow of a person could be clearly seen looking in on us from under the large tree that looms out front. Finding this alone in my office at night gave me cold chills up my spine. I immediately looked at every reference photo I could find that we took of the tree out front to make sure there wasn't a strangely shaped shrub playing tricks on my eyes. There was nothing to be found. Looking through all the subsequent shots of the door, the shadow was not there. Was someone out there messing with us? Did I just capture something paranormal? One thing was for sure, something was there, and I caught it on video.

Unaware of what was captured, we went on with our investigation. Sara was asking several questions and eventually asked:

"Is there anything here that means us harm?" after only a second, a sick feeling came over me as I heard a faint sound in the back corner of the room. Replaying the audio revealed that we did capture something, but it wouldn't be until later that we would be able to really decipher what it was. The EVP was hard to hear without boosting the volume. The sound had been captured right at the 30 Hz frequency. Barely in the range of what falls in the normal spectrum of hearing, but far outside the range of what human vocal cords would produce. Listening to the boosted audio we could clearly now hear the response to Sara's question. The voice said:

"Here" followed by a light-hearted female laugh. On its own did not sound threatening, but when paired with Sara's request to know if there was anything there that wanted to harm us, it gave me a unsettling feeling about everything we had done.

Knowing we had received a response, but not knowing the content at the time, we continued with our session. Sara inquired if the spirit that had just made a sound in the back was the spirit that was responsible for making all the strange noises. Without warning or hesitation, Sara this time heard a voice over her shoulder (that we were unable to capture) followed by three rhythmic banging sounds just outside. Looking out the door to determine the source, at first, she spotted the shadow of a person standing outside. However, as she looked at it, the image disappeared. Unwilling to say that she saw a shadow figure disappear, she insisted that her eyes may have been fooling her. At the time the assessment seemed very logical but, after finding video evidence of a shadowy figure lurking outside the church, we would later question the experience.

Almost on cue, as we were distracted by the sounds outside, I heard a sound from our back corner yet again. This time I was able to identify it as a female voice, even though I couldn't understand what it just said. Immediately checking my recorder revealed the same scenario as before. Audio enhancement would provide a validation to the previous EVP, as this on also fell within the 30 Hz range. A single word called out, this time the name of one of our group members... Sara.

As exciting as everything sounds, at the time things were unfolding at a slow pace and we were unaware of much of our evidence. We sat in the dark listening to the sounds of our own questions, which were growing fewer and further in between. As we were beginning to grow restless and break off into conversation, suddenly and with a start, Allie jumped up from the bench she was sitting on. After several minutes of feeling flustered she finally started to answer my questions about what had happened. Embarrassed, she admitted to us that something had grabbed her... on her butt. We looked all around the area she was sitting looking for branches or some other debris that might have shifted and poked her, but no explanation could be found. As we stood there in wonder, trying to figure out what had happened, I caught something amazing on my camera, once again, without even knowing it.

I would later find that, while standing in the middle of the room watching everyone else mess around with the bench trying to convince ourselves of its instability, I had kept my camera trained on Allie as she watched in horror as each explanation fell apart. As she stood there, I captured frame by frame a piece of her hair being moved delicately off the side of her face and get tucked behind her ear, as if I had reached up to do it myself. Over the course of days, I watched this clip repeatedly trying to debunk the event as the wind moving her hair. However, not only does no other piece of her hair move, neither does Sara's within the same frame. Not to mention that inside the church is no airflow at all. We were all sweating because of the stillness in that room that night. With no amount of convincing that I could give to a viewer about that incident, I know beyond the shadow of a doubt that what happened was not through conventionally explainable means.

Eventually we would wrap up the inside investigation, mostly with a feeling that we had really captured nothing although we had captured more evidence that night than on any other investigation up to that point. We moved into the open field on the opposite side of the church to find the highest levels of consistent EMF spikes we've ever recorded at a location. It didn't take long to figure out that the entire area was surrounded by power lines connected to power boxes. While the readings themselves were perfectly normal for the circumstances, it did bring up the question. Was this high EMF amplifying the paranormal activity at the location? Were we having experiences and feeling paranoid because of the electromagnetic fields wreaking havoc on our bodies?

I certainly came away from the Carter location with a new attitude about what I thought I knew about paranormal investigation. Sometimes the most boring and uneventful night can later turn out to be a treasure trove of evidence. Sometimes you will review your evidence only to come away with even more questions that need to be answered. Any time I find myself bored on an uneventful investigation, I think back to my time at Carter and remember my lesson.

After Dark Paranormal Investigations

Ashton Rogers

SCHRÖDINGERS'S HAUNTING
THE ARLINGTON VISITORS CENTER
Kristin Martindale

Although I'd already been a videographer with NTPI during several prior cases, I was especially excited being able to investigate the Arlington Visitor's Center. It would be my first high-profile case, commissioned by the city of Arlington, and I'd get to branch out and do more than I ever had before. Previously, I was just "Kristin Martindale" the camera operator who followed the team around, watching as a third-party participant. However, I was finally being given more responsibilities and couldn't wait to join the rest of the team in the investigative process. For this case, I had been promoted to the lead equipment technician, running not only my usual camera equipment, but also getting the chance to test out the new static camera system, set up additional audio equipment, and conduct experiments on my own. I couldn't wait to venture out with the rest of the team and discover everything the visitor's center had to offer. As a bonus, we were the only paranormal team to investigate the building, so the pressure was on.

As part of our study, I went into the investigation blind to the history and eyewitness accounts that were experienced at the location. In our process, whenever possible, we try to keep a control group for every investigation, meaning half of us know what to expect going in, and the other half do not. Sara and I were decided to be the control. But, while we had no idea during the investigation, we would later be filled in on the details of this place.

As I would later learn, before the current building was put in place, the land was previously the site of the historical Arlington Downs Horse Track. Waggoner built the track for prize-winning horse races, in which spectators would gamble high amounts of money and partake in all kinds of criminal debauchery. It also held shows, rodeos, and civic events on the property. The racetrack thrived until 1937, until state legislature repealed parimutuel laws and Arlington Downs was sold to commercial developers. It was still used for various events until 1958, when the buildings were raised. The area and current building is now owned by the Texas Rangers Baseball team and sits adjacent to The Ballpark in Arlington.

When we first arrived at the location, the stadium across the street was at the end of a very exciting sportsball game. I, not being one for sports in any way, couldn't tell you at all what had just taken place, but some others in our group seemed surprised that the game had taken so long. There was a ton of traffic, a crowd loitered on the sidewalks, and finding our way into the building was a challenge. However, we would eventually find ourselves on the second-floor lobby with all our equipment and two of the visitor center's own employees, who were eager to share their paranormal experiences with us.

Our primary contacts for this investigation were Nikki and Lauren, two women who worked in the building full-time and were very excited to get started. In 2016, they reached out to us after a mutual third-party met with us at a public appearance in Granbury, Texas. Unfortunately, due to delays caused by scheduling issues on the client's side, we couldn't begin our investigation of the Arlington Visitor's Center until August of 2017. It was then that we were finally able to sit down with these two ladies face to face and learn all about the experiences people were having at the location. While many of the employees at the building were willing to discuss their experiences, not all wanted to be identified, so they were collected and relayed to us by Nikki and Lauren. Later, after we would put our video out, our group would receive emails from the staff further confirming the experiences we would have that night.

Because I was part of our group's control, I would not learn about their experiences until after the investigation was completed. I was quickly learning how hard it was to work on a need-to know-basis. I would be told simply that there were areas with "activity" that we needed to capture and would have to decide on how to place cameras without really knowing what I was looking for. After everything was set up I would check with the lead to see if any adjustments needed to be made.

Nikki, herself, had several experiences in the building. One night, while working alone in her cubicle, she heard and felt a hard *thunk* about twenty feet away, on the other side of the room and out of view. The sound was like boots hitting a hardwood floor, but all the floors are carpeted. She heard and felt footsteps walk around the backside of the office and stop just feet outside the opening of her cubicle. She froze. She knew she was the only one in the building, but after several endless minutes, she carefully peeked out of her cubicle to be sure. When she found no one there, she immediately left without turning off her computer or even looking back.

She went on to tell us about the night a coworker returned to the building to get some paperwork off a desk in the common room area. Nearby, from the closed conference room, she could hear a loud discussion and felt the vibrations of movement, as if a very energetic meeting was taking place with distinctly male voices ringing out. However, when she peered into the conference room windows, she could see that the room was pitch black and empty.

The office manager reported hearing the back door to the stairwell slam shut hard enough to vibrate the walls. It is always when she's staying late, and she has never seen it happen in person. Even after checking the security footage, the door never seems to move. It's only the sound that is heard.

During normal business hours, the bathroom door has locked itself with nobody inside. One day, the employees all found that the door was locked, but the office accounted for everyone in the building. Even going so far as to check the surveillance system to see who might be inside, they found no one had gone into the restroom. After accounting for everyone, the door mysteriously unlocked itself. The deadbolt can only be unlocked with a key from the outside and must be locked from the inside without it.

Many employees and even some corporate visitors reported hearing typing in the office area when nobody is there during all hours of the day. Some feel like they're being watched when downstairs in the warehouse level after hours. Almost everyone agrees that the place feels creepy whenever they're alone. With plenty of eyewitness accounts and many different types of experiences, we were all excited to see what we might find.

As Allie began her interview, Sara and I headed into the break room on the other side of the building, so we wouldn't hear anything. In the break area, we both noticed that the outside noise invaded the room. The sportsball game outside was bleeding through the walls, as well as the voices of people walking down the sidewalk outside of the building. There was absolutely no sound proofing, which was noted for our investigation notes.

After the interview was over, we were fetched from the break room and got to work. I began setting up the static cameras, making sure that we were capturing the two main hallways, the break room, the women's bathroom, and the cubicles. All, of course, without knowing any specifics of what I was trying to capture. Once all the static cameras were set up and ready to go, I grabbed my video camera and started recording.

If there's one thing I have learned from working with this group, it's that redundancy is a lifeline. There's always so much that can go wrong and if you are without a backup you can find yourself in a mess quickly. Allie was equipped with our live-stream camera, and Ashton would take one of the other handhelds with him as usual. I would later be very thankful for having so many backups.

After a brief group meeting, it was decided that we would all split up to different sections of the building. Ashton and Don headed down to the warehouse, I went into the women's bathroom, Allie went to the cubicles with Nikki and Lauren, and Sara would cover the boardroom. Oblivious to what the other groups were doing, I took a seat on the bathroom's sofa and began an EVP session armed with nothing but my camera.

It was pitch black in the bathroom. Even looking through my camera's viewer, it felt too dark due to the small, enclosed space. I was slightly uncomfortable, trying to settle in as I thought up some questions. At first, the questions were basic and uninspired, since I had no clue what to expect. Then I remembered overhearing one of the girls say to be careful, because whatever was here enjoyed scaring women. This gave me the idea to use my gender to coax whatever might have been messing with women to mess with me.

"I hear you like scaring women. Why do you do that?" That warranted no reaction. "Do you dislike women?" Nothing. "Is it funny to scare them?" Silence. This went on for about 15 minutes, the tension building slowly. Finally, I asked, "Well, I'm a woman. Why don't you try scaring me?" Which may have been the beginning of my undoing.

Without warning, my camera shut off. When the light faded from my screen, I was left alone in the complete darkness, the shock of the sudden blackness causing me to panic and rush for the door. I flung it open, thankful for the hallway light on the other side. Hyperventilating, I then turned my attention to my camera. I had been watching the battery as I filmed, and it was full just a few seconds ago. I impatiently turned the power back on and was greeted by a message: "Would you like to recover your data?" I was horrified that my camera footage might be lost, so I pressed accept while hurrying to find Ashton, our other resident tech.

I didn't know it at the time, but I wasn't the only one who had experienced something at that moment in time. It may have been coincidence, but within just a few seconds of each other two other members of the investigation would capture evidence of their own.

While I was in the bathroom, Ashton and Don had headed down towards the first-floor warehouse area. They began checking some of the doors, seeing if they could slam them and make the sound echo. Starting with the back stairwell the found that there was almost no way to make the door slam without applying heavy steady force to it. The door was on a hydraulic designed to prevent exactly that. Eventually they moved on to the downstairs door with much more success. It seemed like they were able to replicate what sounded like the back door banging and concluded at the time that it was possible the manager might be hearing one of the downstairs workers slamming one of those doors when leaving and mistaking it for the stairwell door.

Finally, making their way into the warehouse area, they turned all the lights out, and the eeriness of the warehouse sunk in. Ashton would later describe the cluttered space to me as claustrophobic and constricting. The place was like a serial killer's dreamland. There were tall shelves full of boxes, making every row and every corner a blind one. Walking through the area made you feel uneasy, like something was going to get you around the next corner. It was discomforting.

As they carefully walked through the warehouse, they noticed a loud banging noise directly below the upstairs cubicles. It was there that they discovered the air conditioning unit, which would make a loud bang when it kicked on, followed by a vibration that shook the area around it. This might have explained the sounds of disembodied footsteps in the cubicles upstairs.

Continuing their investigation, Ashton and Don, too, could hear the voices and sounds coming from outside, but only in one area near an outside door made for receiving shipments to the building. Behind the rows and rows of suffocating clutter, they checked out the break area before Ashton discovered an inconspicuous door that led to a small cluster of offices. Entering the area alone (leaving Don by himself in the dark warehouse) he shut the door behind him, and waited for a moment to gauge the level of sound contamination. To his surprise, this area of the building was well insulated against sound. As he briefly moved from office to office he would ask questions into the darkness and pause in silence to record a response. We wouldn't discover until later that he would capture a voice on his audio: "Close the door." At the exact moment he received this EVP was when my camera had shut off upstairs.

Upstairs in the cubicles, Allie sat with Nikki and Lauren, recording an EVP session with the live-stream. Although they didn't get any responses, they did discover later that they would capture an orb on the video that seemed to shoot into Lauren during their session. While we normally discount orbs simply as dust or other debris, it did happen to appear in frame at the same time Ashton got his EVP downstairs and my camera shut off in the bathroom. It wasn't even a piece of evidence that we tagged, but our clients thought that it was of significance. It was also here, near the cubicles, that we discovered an acrylic sign attached to the wall directly beneath an air vent that rattled when the a/c was on, or even when someone walked by. The sound it made was akin to the sound of typing on a keyboard, which was one of the phenomenon Nikki and Lauren had relayed to us in the interview earlier. It was likely that this acrylic sign was the culprit.

As their session was wrapping up, I passed by on my way downstairs and alerted them to my experience in the restroom. Almost as shaken as I was, Lauren visibly jumped into Nikki's arms and immediately asked me where the men had gone. The three of them grouped up with me and headed down into the warehouse.

Unaware of our experiences, in the warehouse. Ashton stepped out of the downstairs offices and found me rushing toward him, begging for help with the camera error – Allie, Nikki, and Lauren all in tow. I began to report what had happened to him as he attempted to fix the malfunction. Later, when we watched this footage, we would note that my southern accent, apparently, becomes very thick when I'm frazzled. As Ashton listened to my story, Donald made an observation: It was as if we had all been corralled into the same area. We'd had this happened once before, at Kyle cemetery. This realization caused shivers up my spine. It was then that he made another observation. Where was Sara?

Sara was in the boardroom doing EVP's alone, unaware that she had been completely abandoned by the rest of us, sitting in darkness. After nearly forty-five minutes of no interaction she decided to come look for us. Walking from area to area she would quickly learn that she was the only one left on the second floor and the feeling was disconcerting. As soon as we noticed and went to find her, we all managed to meet in the stairwell. And, while grouped up in the back stairs, Sara shared a few details about the boardroom with us. When leaning against any part of the wall, it creaked loudly, and she could hear a lot of noise bleeding through from all of us. The way sound traveled in this building was obviously becoming a huge factor in the investigation. Distant noises would sound close-up, and close-up noises would echo in strange ways. She even noted while walking through the cubicle area that she had experienced a sort of "lag" in the sound of her own footsteps. We were finding it very easy for the building to play tricks on the ear even when outside sounds were not a factor.

We decided it was a good idea to regroup so that everyone could take a step back from what had happened so far that night. But, first, Sara wanted to look at the warehouse. So, everyone went upstairs except for her and me. I waited outside of the warehouse, trying to calm my nerves from earlier as I waited patiently for Sara to come back out. Although, once again finding myself alone, even having lights on around me proved to be unnerving, and I counted down the minutes for Sara to come back out the door.

Alone in the warehouse, Sara caught an EVP almost immediately, which sounded like an animal growling from around the serial killer hiding corners near where Ashton had ventured alone. She, then, thought she heard whispering and barking coming from the large room on the other end of the warehouse. Retreating from the dark space, she bumped into a rolling chair and frightened herself, hurrying out to meet me in the stairwell. On review of the video, we did notice something strange about the chair she bumped into. While not a one hundred percent certainty, Ashton would later tell us that, while watching the video, he noticed that during her initial walk past the area, the chair seemed to be up against a small partition area. However, when she walked back, after being startled, the chair seemed to be in the pathway pulled out. Had the chair moved on its own? There's no way to really know for sure, but we did find the placement and timing to be odd. Quickly, Sara exited the warehouse and met up with me on the stairwell. I had no idea what had happened, but noticed that she looked pale and a bit spooked. We decided to head back up to the common room to regroup with the others.

Back in the front lobby, we all took a moment to gather ourselves and share what we'd seen or heard so far on our livestream. As I shared my experience with the camera in the bathroom, Sara became excited and, as usual, was eager to head into the bathroom by herself. Because of the static camera set up in there, we all decided to gather around the portable screen and watch from a distance while she went to the restroom alone. We all watched in silence as we indulged our voyeuristic curiosity of Sara's EVP session. Luckily, we had a new camera system that was equipped with sound, so we could all hear what was going on in real time. We all listened intently and focused, straining to hear or see any form of evidence that there was something in there with her lurking in the dark. I was no longer frightened from the event in there, although I was nervous about the camera malfunction and what I might have messed up.

My first investigation where I had more responsibilities, and I felt like I had already flubbed it up.

After about fifteen minutes passed, almost as if Ashton could sense the uncertainty lingering in the air, he decided to lighten the mood, all while giving us something to laugh about later. As Sara sat in the pitch-black bathroom and asked questions, she had no idea that Allie had urged Ashton to go through with his plan. It wasn't until the door banged opened and she let out a shriek that we all exhaled a breath of relief and reveled in the laughter. You would think we would be more used to this sort of abuse from our lead investigator, but he always knows the right moment to sneak up on us. I'm not sure what perverse joy he gets out of it, but he doesn't even seem phased when it results in him getting punched in the face.

After the tension was lifted, we decided to proceed with the rest of our investigation with newfound excitement. Sara and I went back into the warehouse, venturing further into the darkness this time, daring whatever was there to come out and play. While we didn't have any activity to record, upstairs in the boardroom the rest of the team was having more luck.

While we were in the warehouse, Ashton, Allie, Nikki, and Lauren gathered in the boardroom and began another EVP session as the live-stream watched on. They started by running an SB-7 Spirit Box session in which they listen to radio scans for responses. However, having no real luck, switched back to more conventional means of using a digital recorder. After asking a few questions for thirty minutes, they reviewed the recorded audio live for their audience and found something surprising right before Ashton began talking in one of the strings of questions. The live-stream recognized the word clearly right off the bat, and they couldn't wait until Sara joined them to hear it for herself. Fortunately, they didn't have to wait long, and Sara and I entered the boardroom soon after. Ashton played the audio back for us, and clear as day, we heard "Sara" whispered into the recorder. Although excited, Sara hardly seemed surprised. It was here we noted that many times on investigations, it's her name that we will capture in recordings. We theorize it might be because she is our designated EVP tech and usually does most of the communication.

By the time we'd met in the boardroom and heard Sara's name spoken, it was time to start cleaning up. I recall walking down the long hallways to gather the static cameras and the place feeling a bit eerie. I especially remember grabbing the camera from the bathroom as fast as possible and booking it out of there, afraid something might pop out of the stall to grab me. I felt like I'd had enough fun for one night. After collecting all our equipment, we thanked Nikki and Lauren for having us out and headed out into the parking lot, where only a couple people still lingered from the sportsball game. It was a vast contrast to the large crowd when we'd arrived, which only added to the unsettling feeling I felt.

When I learned about the history of Arlington Visitor's Center and the previous experiences in the car later, all I could think about was the event in the bathroom and immediately started connecting the dots. More than anything, I really hoped the footage wasn't lost. Later, I'd learn that it wasn't lost, but had been corrupted, and therefore unusable. I initially felt like I had failed, but the group reassured me that I had not. Ashton explained that sometimes in science what we perceive as our failures, themselves, are a crucial part of the study and evidence. If what had happened hadn't done so when it did, the other events may not have had nearly as much significance or impact.

I would also later find out that Nikki had emailed us shortly after our visit to tell us about some other strange coincidences going on during the investigation that we didn't even know about. During our investigation, the building security camera would also have a malfunction of its own with no less than five cameras suddenly dropping out for no reason. Also, only days after the investigation, the AC unit would mysteriously stop working. While we didn't get any readings that showed it, I wonder if there wasn't electrical interference causing all our simultaneous phenomenon?

Our conclusions coming away were twofold: Much of the activity could be explained, but some key activity was very much inconclusive. We get asked a lot if a place is haunted or if it's just normal stuff going on. The question I'm starting to ask myself now is: "Why can't it be both?"

THIS WAY TO THE GOATMAN
ALTON BRIDGE

Sometimes the history of a location is lost and completely forgotten, only to be found in dusty history books and lost genealogy records. These ghostly places are a challenge in themselves to investigate when trying to dig up the facts. However, what is more of a challenge is when we find that the history has not been forgotten, but rather, sensationalized to the point that the lines of fact and fiction have become blurred. Old Alton Bridge in Denton, Texas is just such a place. The local legends told today trace back to very real events and people, but the truth has become twisted and embellished over time. So much so, that this location was not just an interesting investigation for our group. But, also attracted the attention of a very popular TV show group as well.

Long before Alton Bridge had received the attention of our

beloved TV group, local paranormal investigators and weekend ghost hunters alike had spent countless weekends trying to capture a piece of the urban legends surrounding the location for themselves. Performing even the most casual of internet searches will result in a hundred pages of links to the history and evidence linked to the Goat-Man and Old Alton Bridge. As I would find, it doesn't take long to get lost in the sea of misinformation out there. Even tagging along on the official tour, the facts were blurred for entertainment value. I would eventually find that I needed to talk to an actual historian, as well as spend some time in the city library, to get to the truth underneath all the stories.

My initial findings turned up a very common story that I have heard several times, always seemingly in locations near an old bridge that is no longer in use. The urban legend says if you knock on the bridge three times at midnight, or turn off your car lights and honk three times, then you just might receive a visit from The Goatman, a half-man half-goat creature with the intent of dragging you to hell. Numerous reports tell of red glowing eyes in the darkness, and sightings of a large humanoid goat-headed beast living in the woods.

It's rumored that these sightings are due to a story predating the bridge. The story supposedly dates to the 1860's. A group of Copper Canyon cowboys are believed to have lynched a runaway Creole slave goat-herder named Jack Kendall from a creek-side tree near where the bridge now stands. But due to their ineptitude, managed to decapitate the man by mistake. Watching in horror, the headless body raised itself from the creek bed mud, through the power of voodoo, and ripped off the head of a nearby goat to replace his own, which was still hanging in the noose.

While the particulars of this legend are quite flavorful, it's not an uncommon one and rarely hold any truth. However, I always feel like some legends do have roots based in fact. It's this thinking and some digging that helped me connect some of the dots to turn up a much more likely story.

In the late 1930's a black entrepreneur named Oscar Washburn ran a farmstead near the bridge. He was well known by the locals for his quality livestock of goats, meat, milk, cheeses and hides. To advertise he hung a sign on the bridge directing "This way to the Goatman," which infuriated local Ku Klux Klansmen and the mayor who plotted violence in collusion. For a few years they would terrorize the family that had made their home just a few miles north of the bridge by posting up in the woods with lanterns calling out threats nightly as they made their way to the small shanty. Finally, one night, a lynch mob stormed Washburn's shack and dragged the screaming man to a noose waiting on the bridge, tightened the rope around Oscar's neck, then pushed him over the side. However, when the men looked to admire their handiwork, they were frightened to find only an empty noose dangling over calm waters.

Panicking, they searched the area unsuccessfully before rushing to Washburn's shanty, setting it ablaze with his family shrieking inside. It was supposed to be a bait to elicit a rescue attempt by the vanished Oscar. However, Washburn was never seen again, his family killed in the fire.

Eventually, word got out about what had happened, and the rumors circulated that the Mayor was somehow involved in the decision to let the Klan do their business without fear of the law getting involved. As the facts turn more into legend, several of the men said to have participated in the botched execution turned up missing never to be found.

While this story is much more believable, it still has holes that cannot be verified by any records. But, many of the local historians agree that there was, in fact, a "Goat-Man" named Oscar who was lynched on the bridge before having his house torched to the ground, giving some weight to significance of the area. What is deeply rooted in fact is that the thickly wooded area around the bridge stretched along Hickory Canon and Copper Creek covers several miles, and over the past fifty years has a very real and documented history of missing persons cases. In the many years following the mysterious disappearance of the Goatman, numerous abandoned automobiles were discovered on or near the bridge. Not only that, but reports of missing persons were made, but no one was ever found. Some of these reports were made in very recent years.

The first night we ever went out to see the bridge, we had a hard time finding it. It is well hidden by trees and an alcove off the main road, but so close you will wonder how you missed it. The main path crossing over the creek runs alongside the modern main road separated only by a metal guardrail and some foliage to give a false sense of seclusion.

As usual, we decided to pre-walk the area and take in the experience of it all to get a feel for the location before getting any kind of equipment out. Walking up to the main trail and approaching the bridge, we couldn't help but laugh as we noticed a rather large group of people gathered on the bridge huddled around a rather colorful piece of paranormal investigation equipment. As we got closer, we realized we had stumbled across someone who was giving a ghost tour. It hadn't even occurred to us that it was getting close to Halloween and that there might be a crowd. Initially we had just planned to politely wait for the group to finish their walk, but we were spotted and invited to join them. Interested in hearing more about the location and watching the guide conduct her investigation, we were eager to tag along.

As the guide told her stories about the experiences people had in different spots on the bridge and along the trail, she would use her colorful EMF detector, recorder, and camera to try to contact spirits. The results seemed random as different parts of the device would light up, but the people on the tour enjoyed the show well enough. She had several stories of investigators and guests that had been scratched, captured images of orbs, and in one case a dark shadow that apparently scared the photographer badly. Once the tour was over, we talked with her a little bit about our group, what we were up to and attempted to get a little more information about the area. She was pleasant, but seemed slightly annoyed by us, as it was getting late and she had just run her last tour for the night. We did manage to find out a few more details that we had not previously been able to come across. In addition to reports of the goat-man, people also reported the apparition of a woman who wandered the woods and the creek in search of her lost children. People have also said that, while hiking in the deeper parts of the woods, they have run across a cabin that they thought might be the old Washburn residence, only to find out later that it no longer exists. Deeming it far too late to get started and put off by nearby teenagers who were partying by the campfire they had just made, we decided it best to come back during a less busy time of year.

On our second trip out, about a month later, we had only

slightly better luck. We quickly learned that there was no such thing as a slow time of year for the popular location. This time we found the lot full of sports cars. Overflow from a nearby car convention and tourists peeking at the famous bridge for themselves. Having driven all the way out to the location from an hour away we decided just to wait until the area had cleared out some before exploring some of the back areas of the woods where we had not been yet.

Our patience paid off. When we re-emerged from the woods we found that the traffic had cleared out. Grabbing some light hand equipment from the car, we began to conduct a small investigation on the bridge just to see if we could document anything unusual. As we left the bridge with our cameras and recorders, we accidentally stumbled onto a group of teenagers who had emerged from the woods looking nervous. Noticing the NTParanormal Investigation logos on our shirts and our equipment they immediately knew what we were doing and began to ask us questions and agreed to participate in an interview with us. Of course, they rehashed all the local legends we had already heard ten times before this. But, we found it increasingly hard to keep straight faces as they recounted the events of that night leading up to our interview.

We learned that we had intercepted them during an expedient retreat from the woods where they had been playing with a Ouija Board out in the woods. After the three boys had been asking some innocuous questions without much of a response, one of them had become brave and started trying to contact the Goat-Man directly. After getting some strange answers from the board they asked the board if there were any other beings out in the woods. The board pointed to *Yes*.

"What are you." One of the boys bravely asked, his hand beginning to shake in the cold. As the planchet began to move on the board it began to spell out a word that made each boy's heart sink.

S-A-T-A-N

Stunned, the boys were afraid to ask anything else and sat in silence for several seconds. Then, without warning, a bush nearby began to violently shake as if something was coming out of the woods to grab them and drag them down to hell. Screaming, the board went flying as they all three ran out of the woods to the main trail. Trying not to look panicked, they had stopped running but were exiting at a quickened pace down the main trail when they had run into us.

By this point, the boys had calmed down from their original scare, and we managed to talk them into taking us back to the location where everything had occurred to investigate and retrieve the Ouija Board. After several minutes of walking, talking, and recording we went back to the spot that they said everything had taken place. We could easily tell that the area had been occupied due to the cleared-out leaves and the cinder blocks positioned in a circle for them to sit.

However, we could not locate the Ouija Board even using our high-powered flashlights and IR cameras. We reasoned that the bush shaking was probably an animal that lives in the woods that they had disturbed and probably took their board to be used as bedding in whatever nest it had made nearby. But, just for our own amusement, we told them that it could also have been the devil and they should probably all go home.

We continued our investigation for another hour on the bridge, but due to the loud traffic and a second set of teens who had come to the bridge to make out, we figured once again that it was late and that we probably would not be able to do a complete investigation any time soon. Deciding that we would return the next year on a weeknight, when the odds would be much lower of running into other people, we packed up our equipment for the night.

We returned the following year in July with a little more equipment, a new team member, and knowledge that there were no events going on nearby this time of year. We also made sure that it was a miserably hot weeknight to discourage the chances of anyone thinking the woods would be a good place to hang out for the night. As another precaution, we decided to start our actual investigation portion of our trip a bit later than normal. All things that paid off in spades, as we found we would be the only people there for the whole night.

This time we started at the pavilion area near the benches and the beginning of the hiking trail. The absence of traffic made the experience much more surreal. Not being able to hear the occasional car go by really added to the feeling of seclusion, even though we all knew the main road wasn't far away. Gathering around to do an EVP session, we recounted how a woman claimed to have taken a photograph of a Klansman's shadow at this very spot where she also received three scratches on her arm shortly after. Sara began asking questions while I took readings on my EMF detector and the others took pictures. I asked for whatever was there push, scratch, and shove me. But, we never captured anything in that area that we couldn't explain.

After wrapping up at the benches, we decided to walk the long trail into the woods. We wanted to use up some of our time until midnight when it was said that the activity would really ramp up on the bridge. We found it strange that as soon as we crossed the threshold of the trail gate, the mood suddenly seemed to shift. Two of the cameras that I had just put fresh batteries into suddenly was giving messages of needing replacements, while one of our flashlights also seemed to be malfunctioning. Luckily, we weren't far from the car, so I was able to get replacements into the equipment quickly, so we could continue with the investigation. It was strange that three pieces of equipment all seemed to malfunction at the same time, but we didn't get any other activity along with it to suggest that it might be paranormal in nature. We simply noted in our logs and continued, not realizing how significant the event would be later.

Starting again, Sara, Allie and I all decided to continue down the main trail. Don, feeling brave, decided that he wanted to split off and try to get pictures and illicit a response on the bridge by himself. On that note, we parted ways and the rest of us made our way down the trail. Not making it a full hundred feet down the pitch-black path, Allie began to get nervous and told me that she felt like we were being watched. Not uncommon in a dark wooded area, but we understood what she was talking about. Something about this was different than what we had experienced before. It was heavy, thick, and impending. After some coaxing, Sara was able to get her to keep moving forward deeper into the dangerous feeling.

After about a sixth of a mile, the trail dumped out into a clearing behind everything. The feeling here was less oppressive and better illuminated. There is a church about a quarter of a mile in the distance on the other side of the clearing that bathed the area with its flood lights, making it much easier to see and navigate. We had learned on the previous tour that this area was known for producing the smell of onions that were supposedly sold by the wife of Oscar Washburn off a wagon style cart. While none of us ever did smell anything in the area, we did note that onions grew wild in the area, so this was probably just another rumor that was thrown out there to get their group excited about the idea of a possible paranormal encounter. As we made our way through the area, we tried to elicit responses on our SB-7 and our recorder, but didn't seem to have any luck.

As we pushed forward, the area began to grow darker as we moved out of the reach and safety of the church's flood lights. As we grew more isolated, things began to get more tense. Leading the group, I scanned the area for anomalies using my infrared thermal camera. I called out to the group, who were a few paces behind me, telling them to be quiet, when I thought I heard something in the brush beside me. My initial reaction was that it was an animal rustling around. However, when I pointed the thermal camera in that direction I couldn't see anything. Normally animals show up bright yellow in orange due to their heat signature. Uneasy I froze, leaning toward the darkness and called out.

Eyes fixed on the camera screen, I gasped in fright as I saw a blue and purple cold spot move towards me along the ground. Quickly, I stepped back, stumbling and almost falling as it moved towards my direction. Immediately, I brought up my flashlight to get eyes on whatever it was that was about to attack me. The rest of the group just stood on the trail and waited to watch death drag me away into the woods. As my light scanned the area in front of me, I found myself relieved as I could finally see the source of my anomaly. Although educated, I am not well versed in animal biology. As it turns out, while armadillos do carry as much body heat as other warm-blooded creatures, it's hidden by their thick shell. Thus, making them look like strangely demonic shaped and clumsy cold spots that lumber around on the ground. Exclaiming my need for a change in pants, I let the girls catch up to me and put Sara in the lead.

We continued through the wooded trail farther down hickory creek than we had ever ventured in the dark, leaving all signs of civilization far behind us. Even after nearly two miles of rough hiking, we did not see any sign that the trail would loop around or end. We had hoped to maybe catch a glimpse of the legendary cabin, but sadly it never appeared. We decided to sit in a small circle on the trail and run an EVP session while we rested for the trip back, and while we did not receive a response on our recorder, something about being alone that deep in the woods felt unsettling to me. Even being an avid camper used to spending the night far off in isolation, something about this place made me feel wholly uncomfortable.

We hiked back along the trail to the entrance, where we finally met back up with Don, who had been investigating the bridge. While we had no luck on our trip, Don was quite excited to tell us about his last hour. After taking several shots with his DSLR, near the entrance and at the rest area, he moved on to the bridge shortly after we split off. Being on his own made him feel quite a bit more uneasy about the location but he pushed on anyway, hoping the fear would provoke a response. After setting up on the bridge he found that his camera was no longer working. He tried several things to find that the shutter was not responding. He was reading that he had plenty of battery power, his viewfinder was working properly, and by all indications should have been able to take pictures. But, after fifteen minutes of messing with the equipment and a battery change, he could not get the camera to fire at the location. In frustration, Don went back to the car to take a closer look at the equipment in the better lit setting of the SUV. When he got back and retried the camera for a test shot, suddenly, without having done anything, the camera operated normally.

Don took several test shots, and everything seemed to be fine. He decided to take a short break at the vehicle to reorganize some gear in the car. Figuring the shutter must have just has a piece of grass or something stuck in it that had been dislodged, he once again went by the bridge to try again. From twenty feet back, he managed to snap several good pictures of the bridge and documented the surrounding area. However, as soon as he crossed the threshold of the bridge, he would once again find his camera malfunctioning. He would spend another forty minutes trying to figure out if he had messed up a setting in the dark. It was about this time that he had heard us talking in the distance and would walk back to meet us halfway. The camera would not work again for the rest of the night and I was afraid that the expensive equipment may somehow be damaged. Although, I would find out later after getting home it would function just fine and the batteries were only half way drained. We never did come up with a solid explanation for why that camera was malfunctioning that night, since none of our other camera equipment seemed affected.

We spent the next few hours investigating the bridge area. Being our newest toy, we spent a long time using the SB-7 spirit box to try to get a response. This is a device that quickly scans through radio frequencies and creates white noise that supposedly spirits can communicate through. In my experience,

I find that the device in its default state just picks up interference from local radio stations and short-wave broadcasts. To try to cut down on this, I have modified ours by removing the antenna and shortening the bands in which it cycles. While we still get interference from time to time at high elevations, I find that the they are much easier to identify. However, on this night, something strange did come through.

"So, there was a lynching on this bridge, what can you tell us about that?" Sara asked. I let the box run its cycle through the stations one time. Nothing. "What is your name?" She asked. Once again, I activated the box and let it run, this time about half way through the band a strange sound came through. Almost certainly a voice, but I couldn't understand what it said at the time. Surprisingly at the time this happened, an orb can be seen flying through the shot, however being outside with an IR light that could have been anything. Listening to the recording of the voice later, I would just barely be able to make out what sounded like the name Stephen, but I wouldn't swear on it in court. Only after sharing the evidence with several people would I later hear that the name had shown up in several recordings. Many believe that it is the name of one of the Klansmen that took part in the lynching of Oscar. What makes the evidence compelling is that we continued this session for a long time after the one response and several cycles through bands, we never once picked up any more sounds or traces of radio stations. This means either the response was a very well timed and coincidentally relevant transmission, or something there was trying to answer our question.

Moving on from the SB-7, Sara took some time to investigate the far end of the bridge by herself. Taking only a camera, recorder, and a flashlight, she started taking a more energetic and confrontational angle to her approach. Near the area where many people claimed to see a shadowy figure and sometimes a goat creature, Sara began challenging the entity to show itself. As she snapped pictures and talked with authority, she began to feel like she might not be alone. Turning to her right, a large shrub by itself caught her eye as it seemed to shake. Confident that it was a small animal, Sara stepped forward to investigate. As she moved the branches out of the way, expecting a rabbit or other small creature to appear, she found nothing that could explain the shaking. She stepped back proclaiming to once again shake the bush, so she could get a picture, to be rewarded with a violent shake on command. After snapping a quick picture, she once again moved in to inspect to find nothing. Only when she heard a growling noise from behind her did she get scared enough to move away from the area.

Running back to the group on the other side of the bridge, she told us about the incident and we immediately followed her with the thermal camera. No dark spots or hot spots could be found. Even if an animal had been there and moved from the area, there should have been a trace of heat left behind from where it had been sitting. While we all reasoned that it was probably an animal or maybe an air current, we all still had a sick feeling in our guts about the situation. It closely mirrored the story we had here on our previous trip and the word Satan was on the tips of our tongues.

To wrap up our investigation we took several photos of the surrounding areas and caught images of the lights that many report seeing in the woods. While we couldn't verify every one of them, we were able to determine that the great majority of them were headlight reflections coming off the highway that seems so far away. The movement of the cars make for an eerie presentation and was certainly unnerving. We also found that, even though we thought we were alone, moving down below the bridge near the water's edge revealed that there were, in fact, a few fishermen further down the creek who were working by lantern light. It's very possible that their conversations and lights would interfere with a visitor's communion with ghosts of the past.

When I initially came to Alton bridge, I was excited to experience the legends for myself, but I was also excited to tie them back to the stories they were rooted in. For me, learning the real history is every bit as exciting as the investigation itself. Sadly though, I would find that others would only look to exploit the location to profit from its very rich history.

Some months after we would release the video of our investigation, our beloved TV show group would also release theirs. What we hadn't known was that they had done their investigation about two months before us and were in the stages of producing their episode to air while our investigation was underway. Since we aren't a studio with a large budget, at the time, our turnaround was much shorter for putting videos up on YouTube.

It's hard not to be a bitter about some situations, although I'm trying. At the time I saw the episode air, I had been somewhat a fan of the show. But, seeing how they treated the facts after having been to the same location, interviewed the same people, and experienced some of the same things severely changed the way I saw them. I had always suspected that big studio investigators stretched the truth or over exaggerated a bit for ratings, but I never really considered that they were outright misrepresenting their evidence so badly. Three of the witnesses included people that we had talked to, one of them being the woman who ran the haunted tour. I was shocked at how much her story seemed to change from the one she had told us while standing on site. No doubt they were coached to make the accounts sound scary, but I'm still disappointed at the lack of integrity that was displayed.

The investigation part of the episode was great. It played out much like a cliché horror movie, complete with a demonic oppression and a summoning. The group claimed that the location was deep in the woods, isolated from everything. But, anyone who's lived in Denton knows the reality of the main road not but ten or twenty feet from the bridge. Startling pictures of glowing eyes and orbs in the woods were easily recognizable as the car lights we had captured. Rocks were thrown, a spell was cast, and one of their crew members had a full-blown melt down when the Goatman attacked her spiritually.

What bothered me the most was not that they fabricated a show designed for scares to get ratings. It's that the location had plenty to offer in the way of real evidence and the factual history is good enough to stand on its own without the expensive production. It has taken me a few years to stop fuming over the mistreatment of this historical treasure. While not much happened to us while we were out there, it was still enough that we found the place interesting. One day I would like to go back with a more experienced eye to see what else there is to discover.

For me, the truth is even better than the local stories, but for others, the legends will never die.

Ashton Rogers

SINCE TEXAS BECAME TEXAS
THE HOLDER ESTATE

January 28th, 1998 - Having just finished yet another shouting match with his wife Patricia, Donald Martin slumped over in his work shed smoking a cigarette and tried to calm down to process what he had just heard. As he took several drags from his Marlborough, his blood continued to boil. *Who the hell did she think she was?* He thought to himself. Exhaling the smoke, and not feeling any better, he pocketed the .45 caliber handgun he had been loading and prepared to go back into the house.

Before he could leave the shed, the door opened, and he was met by Patricia's tears and ragged voice telling him he needed to leave. His abusive temper had become out of control, and she was would be leaving that night. Without a word, he stepped toward Patty and put her into a choke hold. Dragging her a few feet into the middle of the shed, he forced her down to the floor crying. Pulling the .45 from his pocket he fired a single shot to the back of her head, killing her instantly.

Leaving the body where it fell, he made his way into the house and back to his step-son Chris' room. Chris, not knowing that his mother had just been executed, didn't know what was coming. Making the nineteen-year-old boy face the wall, Donald put the gun to the back of the teenager's head and fired. As he exited the room he spotted his step-daughter, Ashley, running from the room to investigate the sound. In a swift motion he grabbed the fourteen-year-old girl by the hair and held her firmly in place telling her to *shut up*. When she did not comply, he punched her in the face to get his point across, but underestimating his strength knocked her out. He let her limp body drop to the floor. Not wanting her to miss the terror of knowing she was about to die, he decided to tie her hands and gag her, so she couldn't get away when she woke up.

While Donald waited for his other son to get home, he turned on the police scanner that he kept in the house. He wasn't sure if anyone had heard the shots and called the police. Within a few minutes he heard a dispatch to a house a few doors down from his own. Deciding that it was too risky to stay put, he carried Ashley to the car and fled the scene.

Carlos, the other boy, entered the house. He was nervous because he was past curfew and his step-dad was well known for his temper and punishments. Realizing the house was empty, eventually he made his way to his older brother's room to see what was going on. Devastated by the discovery of his brother's dead body, he called the police. When they arrived on the scene it was only a short amount of time before his mother's body was also discovered. However, it would be more than twenty-four hours before either Donald or Ashlee would turn up.

The next day, in Eastland Texas, the body of a man with a self-inflicted gunshot wound from a .45 caliber handgun to the left temple was found slumped over in a van. Other than the weapon, the only other thing found in the vehicle was a cassette recorder with a chilling message recorded in a cold and calculating tone.

"This is Don... My wife finally told me today she was leaving. To be blunt, she told me she was just using me for the last six years. She told me she was going to take me for everything I've got. I really don't feel any remorse. I know that sounds terrible. My only regret is the 17-year-old. I didn't know where to pick him up... I was going to kill him too, but I didn't get the chance. I shot her in the head, She's in the tack room... I shot Chris, the oldest one, 19 years of age, He's in the bedroom. I shot Ashley Foster, my stepdaughter. I went out the Lipan Highway... After the Stroud Creek entrance, take the next dirt road to the right. I forget the name of it. She's laying in front of an oil lease gate. That's where you'll find her." That's where the tape ended. When the police went to the location they found the tied up and beaten body of the fourteen-year-old Ashley, right where the tape had said, with a single gunshot wound to her head.

May 14th, 2016 - As a paranormal investigator, I research and investigate my fair share of strange and bizarre things. But, I have to say that the most interesting aspect of my job has to be the people that I meet along the way. From witches and psychics to scientists, the most fascinating people to me will always be the clients I interact with. Jane was far from the exception to this rule. Loud, outspoken, a thick southern accent and dripping with personality. The animated way she told us her stories firmly cements her in my mind as one of our most memorable clients.

After seeing us talk at a paranormal expo, Jane contacted me in the fall to discuss the possibility of an investigation at a property she owned in Lipan Texas. Earlier that year she took some photos of a friend near the entrance gate of a private road leading up to her property and found strange results in the pictures. After looking over the photos she sent to me, I had some ideas about what could be going on, but nothing I could say for sure without going out there for myself.

As I talked with Jane over the phone, I learned that the gate in the pictures she sent me was actually quite infamous. It was the same gate that the fourteen-year-old Ashlee Foster had been murdered and left tied up to be found by police the next day. I also discovered that the attached property had been in her family for over 150 years since Texas was first declared a U.S. state. It had also been the site of *The Last Indian Massacre of Hood County.* Eventually after a long discussion she invited us out for an investigation and we set up a date to meet her out there.

Even though I had been warned over the phone, I had no idea what I was in for. Jane had mentioned that, while I could probably get to the property in my car, I should probably bring a truck. Not thinking too much of it at the time, I made the brilliant decision to show up in my compact Kia Spectra thinking I didn't mind a few scratches and dings from brush on the already ten-year-old car. What I hadn't realized was that the private road leading up to the property literally took you through the nearby creek and up a steep rocky incline.

Ultimately a climb that would rip off the back bumper of my vehicle. A bit more than a ding, but the damage had already been done so we just taped it back on and continued with the investigation.

We arrived at the property about an hour before sundown, taking daytime photographs and video for reference. The property was breathtaking. Nestled on one-hundred and sixty acres of land miles from civilization, we felt truly isolated. On the front side of the property was thick trees densely scattered between Robinson creek and the part of the property with the family homestead. In the area we would be conducting the bulk of our investigation sat a house that had been standing since the 1840's. As Jane would tell us.

"It was built by my great, great grandfather and it's been in my family since Texas became Texas. The part still standing is the original property, and the parts that were added on aren't standing anymore." She would say with a proud southern drawl. To many it would just look like a dilapidated house in bad need of demolishing, but we all saw a beautifully preserved piece of history. The wood on the outside was gray with faded white paint, worn from a century of weathering. The front side of the house had been completely torn off by a bad storm the year before we got there, but the central house was still intact. Jane warned us that we had to be careful walking around in the house because it was unsafe, but we couldn't stay out of it. We had to explore. All that remained of the house were the four main rooms, one of which was a main living area complete with an old wood burning fireplace original to the property and still standing strong. Old furniture abandoned to time laid rotting in some of the rooms but added to the creepiness as the sun was setting.

In the front lawn of the house was a hand dug well lined with large chunks of limestone. Looking down into the well it seemed like you were staring into a long dark tunnel. The small amount of water at the bottom reflected our faces back at us, and strange feeling of being watched from another dimension.

A small fence separated the house and well area from a dense collection of trees located just the opposite side. As we were directed over there we learned that the small wooded area held a closely guarded secret. It was a hidden family graveyard. While Jane knew that she had relatives buried on the property, they hadn't been sure exactly where. A few months before capturing the images that she would ask us to analyze, and would ultimately bring us out there, they had begun to clear the trees and brush out of the area. Almost immediately after beginning the project they would find the first grave followed by a few more. The trees and brush were so dense that they were unable to complete the task, but estimated that there were roughly fifteen graves located within the small area. As we cut our way into the thick parts and pushed our way in to get a better look, Sara made a startling discovery that surprised even Jane: There were six graves that were unusually small stones with etchings on them. Closer inspection revealed that each one was an infant's grave all from the same date. Reading off the date written on the stones made Jane pause for a moment before she replied.

"Those must be from the fire when the back part of the house burned down." She had known that some of her family, including several of the children, had died in a house fire around the year 1870, but there had never been records to confirm. We were looking at the evidence that they had never been able to quite piece together. It was an amazing feeling to help someone connect with their own history in that way. Looking at more of the graves we counted seventeen, many of which Jane did not recognize the names but would write them down for later research.

On the back part of the property was a barn and windmill. We were able to check out the outside, but the inside was occupied by things that the family were storing so was considered off limits for our investigation. As we were wrapping up the daylight tour and filming we began our interview with Jane, who would tell us about the historical significance of the geographical location we were at.

The area that we had traversed with my car was called Rough Country Road, which passed right over Robinson Creek. Jane told us of an experience that she had at the location, in which, while driving through the area her and her husband got a flat tire. That far out, cell service is nonexistent, and both were in for a five mile walk before they would be able to make a call. As they made their hike through the area, she commented to her husband that something didn't feel right. She felt like something in the distant past had happened there, but wasn't sure what it was and knew she didn't want to be in the area alone at night. Later that week, bothered by the feeling she had, she would end up doing research on Robinson creek to find that it was quite famous in the local history books.

As it turned out, the area in which you pass over the creek on Rough Country Road is known as Star Hollow. This is significant because one of the most important events in Lipan history took place there. The fight that took place there was called various names by historians. The battle was known as the "Point of Timbers Fight," "Battle of Lookout Point," or the "Ravine

Slaughter." The fight began on September 11th and extended into September 12th during the year 1869.

After some Caddo Indians robbed clothes off a line in town, many of the citizens grew angry and wanted someone to deal with the ongoing native problem and to set an example. Several men from Weatherford and Thorp Springs formed a posse to track down the American Indians. Eventually they caught up with the Native Americans and ambushed them at the creek. The skirmish lasted several days and eventually ended up in Star Hollow as the natives tried to make an escape and unknowingly boxed themselves in. After it got dark it started raining, the white men gained the advantage and finished the fight shooting the natives down. To set an example, they scalped the raiding party including the female squaw that had been with them. This would become the last Indian fight in Hood County.

Jane also told us of another experience she had over by the well. Knowing that her great-great grandfather had dug the well, she had tried to ghost hunt the property herself in the past. Not getting much activity, she made a snarky comment about how easy it would be to dig a well like that. After getting a strange feeling, she turned and snapped a picture, capturing a large green orb.

Excited to get started, we set up static cameras with a monitor throughout the house run off a battery backup. With our camera system we were able to simultaneously capture video from all four rooms of the house over the course of our entire six-hour investigation. Immediately, we noticed a high amount of dust contamination floating throughout the house, which was to be expected. This just meant that orb evidence would only be valid if it showed as an anomaly during our multiple

Monowavelength experiments. What we were really interested in doing was documenting our investigation and possibly capturing shadows or apparitions.

Getting all our other gear unpacked and ready, before we could even start, we began to experience activity that we just couldn't explain. At first, we had tuned it out as the sounds of plumbing in the house until we all suddenly realized, seemingly at the same time, that we were in the middle of nowhere and the house not only didn't have active plumbing; but no plumbing at all. It seemed so stupid that we were immediately intrigued at what the hell was going on. From the back room, seemingly from the wall, was the sound akin to rushing water through a pipe. Knocking, pushing, and listening, the sound continued and seemed to react to our prodding to the point that it was becoming unnerving. It was if the house was breathing... loudly. Using the thermal camera, we couldn't track anything in the wall and were genuinely perplexed until, all the sudden, we heard the sound move from one side of the room to the other by way of the attic. Immediately, we all began to track the sounds that were growing louder. What first sounded like water, then heavy breathing, was becoming a frightening hissing sound. It became clearly apparent that the sound was an animal that we had agitated, as whatever it was began visibly stomping around in the attic above us, causing the ceiling to bow overhead.

No longer afraid of something paranormal going on, we were apprehensive that there might be a dangerous predator in the attic waiting to tear us apart. The area was no stranger to wild cats and other various creatures waiting to drag you away in the night. For the next ten minutes I would try to position myself in a way that I could get a shot of the animal through the ceiling with my thermal camera, just to know what we were dealing with. I secretly hoped that we had cornered the legendary Chupacabra, but I was pretty sure we were just going to find an opossum due to the strange hissing sound it was making. After having no luck, Jane finally decided that she would climb onto a bucket and stick her head up there, despite my hesitation about the plan. Allie was sure that we would be fleeing as a headless corpse dropped to the floor.

With bated breath we waited for Jane to relay the information as she looked around with a flashlight. We all jumped out of our skin as she shouted out:

"What the fuck is that?!" Immediately jumping down from the bucket and just exclaiming. "It's not an opossum! Whatever it is, it's weird!" Of course, having no fear, Sara next decided that she was going to climb up there. Handing her the camera also fitted a thermal, she poked her head up and finally captured an image of the beast. What we couldn't identify with the naked eye and a flashlight in the dark showed up clear as day on the camera. What we had found was a juvenile turkey vulture still covered in its white albino fur and hissing loudly at Sara, who was now encroaching on its space.

After a small reprieve, we were able to back off long enough for the poor animal to finally calm down, so we could continue our investigation. We moved one of our static cams up into the attic area to kept careful notes of where the animal was after that, as to not confuse any sounds or movements that it was making with any of the other evidence that we might tag. While the rest of us moved on to the well to do an EVP session, we left Allie alone in the house to take pictures with the monowavelength camera.

Running the EVP session at the well was an exercise in patience for Sara in particular. Sometimes, on these cases, we must remind ourselves that the host usually won't have the experience that we do at conducting investigations. Even though we had given instructions, Sara would find that Jane would talk out of habit after questions as we were trying to get responses. Several times I looked over and I could see her doing her usual silent count of ten, mouthing out the numbers. But, by the look on her face, I think she was starting to count out of frustration. As with most investigations, our host lost interest after a while and let us start investigating on our own for a while. We spent about another hour asking questions at the well and taking pictures with no results that we considered paranormal. What we did find, however, was that there were large trees that encroach on the area. While we couldn't reproduce Jane's image at the time, through experiences we had on other investigations we were able to make an easy deduction about her green orb.

On humid and damp days, when there's a lot of moisture in the air, it's very common to take pictures of that moisture and it appear as an orb. Typically, those orbs will either show up white or will reflect some of the colors of the surrounding area. Often, when we photograph water and dew falling from a tree, they will appear as green orbs. Based on this info, I asked Jane if she remembers what the weather was like the day she caught the orb photo by the well. Surprisingly, she said she remembered it well because her shoe had gotten stuck in the mud from how wet everything was. Apparently, it had rained the day before and on the day, she took that shot it had drizzled a little that morning. I explained my theory and she confirmed that it was a sound analysis and accepted the explanation.

Moving on to the other side of the fence, we once again attempted to push our way into the small cemetery barricaded by a fortress of branches and brush. Being a bigger guy, I had too much trouble trying to get in. However, Sara being vigilant found a small tunnel beneath all the vines and brush and managed to squeeze into the small space. Passing her equipment through the trees and vines, she began to conduct an EVP session and take readings. As Sara asked questions and notated no changes in EMF, we suddenly got a call over the walkie-talkie. As Allie started to tell us what was going on through the device, suddenly we heard her instantly abandon the walkie-talkie in favor of screaming directly across the open field. We could hear her pleas for help in the distance, but could not make out exactly what she was saying. Afraid an animal may have wandered up to the property, I ran back to the house, immediately leaving the group behind in the dark with a single flashlight and some camera equipment.

As I ran back, I heard Allie scream out again, but this time I was close enough to understand what she was saying to me.

"Hey, come back. There's something moving around in here, right now and it's not the damned bird!" She was waving a flashlight as if it were an S.O.S. beacon at me as I ran through the unfamiliar terrain, almost breaking my neck. Finally, out of breath, I climbed into the house from the ledge that was where the front entrance used to be before it had been taken by a tornado. "Shhhhhh." Allie demanded. "Do you feel that?" She asked with wide-eyed excitement.

Standing still, I tried to hold my breath after having just ran for what felt like a mile. Amazingly I was able to hear and feel what she was talking about. Quickly I checked the static cam that Allie had been staring at as well. The bird was not moving or making any kind of noises. In fact, there was nothing in the attic doing anything. Still being quiet, I looked up from the monitors just in time to hear the rhythmic sound of walking on board to our left. Taking note of everything, we followed the sound as it walked from the main hallway and seemed to move into the main living room area and continue through to the back room before it stopped on its own. Allie and I both looked at each other, frozen, trying to figure out what it could possibly be other than paranormal activity. Finally, able to talk, Allie asked if it could be an animal under the house rather than on it. Considering the possibility, I agreed that it very well could be, but there was no way I was climbing down there to find out.

When the others returned, we told them what had happened. Using the camera rig on a stick we were able to look under the house. While we did find a considerable sized crawl space under the house, we did not track any traces of heat consistent with animal activity. However, that didn't mean that Allie's explanation couldn't be right. The animal could have moved away from the house or simply was hidden under some debris that blocked out its heat source. Without someone crawling down there, which we decided was too unsafe to risk, we would just have to tag the event as unconfirmed but probable as animal activity.

Almost as if something was listening and waiting to prove us wrong, the activity started up again. This time with all of us spread out through two of the rooms. The stepping sounds moved directly past me and straight towards Allie, who was becoming uneasy at the idea that something was moving towards her in the main hallway. Once again looking under the house as the sound was going on, we could not see any traces of heat indicating an animal. Just as suddenly as it had started, the activity stopped. The event itself was exhilarating because it might have been paranormal, however it was frustrating because there was simply not enough data to really confirm it either way. In my head I'm almost positive that it was the movement of an animal, but there was just nothing to support that theory any more than the idea that it could have been a ghost. When the activity didn't start back up again, we decided to move on. Begrudgingly, I had to mark down the event as inconclusive even though we had all been there to witness it. As much as I love to capture possible paranormal activity, I hate marking something inconclusive when I feel like it has a logical explanation.

Thinking that the energy from all the events might help fuel more activity, we decided to start running experiments in the house. Using a digital recorder and our handheld cameras, Sara ran EVP sessions in each room one-by-one. Using a standard list of control questions, seemingly we didn't get any responses. However, near the end of her questions in the front bedroom, Sara let her husband Stephen, who was filming at the time, try some questions based off the history of the property.

"Do you remember when the house was built?" He asked, and received an audible response that sounded much to us like a moaning sound of someone in pain. I called out the noise from behind him, asking if anyone else had heard it to. Stephen asked if the entity would confirm if it had made a noise, and we would hear the same sound again. Both times the sound was caught on the recorder that was being used at the time. We wouldn't hear the moaning sound again.

After several more questions, Sara tried an alternate method of confirmation. Hoping the entity would mimic her, she knocked on the wood frame of the house asking the entity *to please knock back*. Surprised, we all tried not to gasp as we immediately heard two faint knocks in the room directly beside us. I quickly checked the camera to see if our upstairs guest had moved, but he seemed to be sitting tight. Stephen checked the other room to see if maybe Sara's knocking had vibrated something and made it shift in the other room. However, there was so much stuff in there we could not visually confirm at the time and had to move on. Checking the footage from the static camera pointed in that room did not reveal anything shifting during the reply knock. The investigations were beginning to show some promise.

Hoping that the activity in the house was ramping up we decided that it would be a good time to conduct a spirit box session. What was great about the location was that we were so far out in the middle of nowhere that the SB-7 on several test passes was picking up absolutely no radio stations or interference on the much stronger FM band. We set up in the living room and sat in a circle to try to get some responses to questions drawn from the history of the location feeling like we were having more luck with them. For half an hour we asked questions and listened to the box pump out uninterrupted empty static. Just as we were getting ready to give up, Sara checked her notes. She had written down several of the names from the headstones in the graveyard. One-by-one she started asking if any of them were there and wanted to talk to us. Finally, she got to a name from one of the stones Jane had not been familiar with.

"John McKenzie, how old were you when you died?" Sara asked. After 30 minutes of no transmission over multiple sweeps we heard two words come through over two statin sweeps.

"I didn't." I almost didn't catch it and had to do a double take. I asked if it could repeat its answer because I missed what it said. Once again, on a completely different station, the same words "I didn't" came through. Not getting any more responses after that, I would later check the footage to confirm we had heard what we thought we heard. Although a little hard to hear, the words were clear. I wonder what this response could mean and if it's truly paranormal. Did John McKenzie not know he was dead, or was he somehow trying to tell us something else and we simply just don't understand?

Once again, we decided to leave Allie with the static cams alone while we went off to run experiments by the old windmill. After twenty minutes it seemed like history was repeating itself as Allie began screaming over the walkie-talkie. This time it was loud and clear. She was hearing the footsteps, louder and harder this time. As she was talking, she demanded that one of us return right then because the whole house had just banged hard as if someone had just jumped down into the middle of the floor next to her. This time Jane went back while we finished up our experiment.

When we returned to the house, Allie was done. Tired of being left there alone, she wanted a chance to explore the other parts of the property before we moved on to the gate. Stephen and I stayed behind and did EVP's at the house while the girls went to explore the property. We did note that there were several mice running around that did make some strange noises, but nothing like the heavy footsteps and the giant thumping sound that Allie had described. When the girls returned, having captured no further activity, we decided to pack the gear back up and head towards the entrance gate a few miles down the road where Ashley's body had been found and Jane had snapped her images.

After a slow drive back to the entrance fence, I once again got out to evaluate the damage of my car. The rear fender was dragging on my tire and I was frustrated as I was calculating the dollars it was going to cost me to fix the damage It had been caused by my own stupidity. Nonetheless, I started unpacking some hand-held equipment, so we could wrap up our experiments for the night. Pulling up the original images she had sent me on my phone, we spent a good amount of time trying to recreate the images.

In both shots Jane had captured what appeared to be streaks of energy that seemed to surround her friend who was near the gate. One yellow and one white. Initially I thought that one of them was easily debunked as an out of focus vine that had been hanging in the shot, but no matter how I tried I could not get any of the foliage nearby to cause the same effect. Only one time did I come remotely close, but the pattern of the plant just did not make any sense.

Switching gears, we played with the idea that it might have been a bug streaking across during the time she was taking a picture. While this seemed like a logical explanation, since there were insects flying around, after taking nearly fifty pictures of bugs from various positions and recreating the lighting Jane had used when taking the pictures, we could not come up with anything similar. In fact, the out of focus bugs and streaked bugs looked more like shadows than the strange multi-colored lights that Jane had photographed.

We looked for everything we could think of that might be a

reflective surface or artifact in the shot, including the positioning of the vehicles, and came up empty-handed. What I initially thought would be a simple answer had no explanation at all. We concluded the night with an EVP session by the gate with an interesting result. Jane was asking questions at the fence and had mixed up some details of the story. She confused the name of Ashley's brother, Chris, with "David" asking:

"Are you David's sister?" While we didn't hear it at the time the recorder did pick up a response that I would later find in my review of the audio. Right at 31 Hz, near the lower end of the spectrum of human hearing, a soft answer to Jane's question can be heard. A small female voice saying...

"No." Seeing as how Jane had said the wrong name. This answer is relevant to the question. Could this have been the spirit of Ashley Foster reaching out to us?

With so much activity at the Holder estate, it should be easy to conclude that location was experiencing paranormal activity. While I truly believe that it is entirely possible that could be the case, there are many factors that keep us from fully validating this conclusion. For one, we know for sure that there were animals present during the investigation. While we confirmed the location of one particularly noisy guest and were able to keep an eye on him, what other creatures were lurking in the building that we just couldn't see? While we certainly did our best to debunk animal activity, it would be irresponsible to say that there is no way that wildlife didn't contaminate our evidence and experiences. Knowing how far out in undeveloped area we were, thinking that there aren't animals calling those structures home would be amateur indeed.

Having said that, much of our audio evidence does support the idea that, not only is there paranormal activity at the location, but that it might be intelligent. Knocks and voices displaying the recognizable characteristics of human speech inside and outside the range of human vocal cords, as well as, being inside and outside the range of human hearing make for fantastic evidence. Once again, these could be the sounds of animals, which have been known to make noises that sound like speech. However, the haunting voice received through our spirit box that was seemingly intelligent lends some weight to the idea that our sounds were not the work of animals.

While I won't commit to telling anyone that the Holder estate was, without a doubt, haunted. There is certainly evidence to suggest that the history of the property is still with it and receptive to visitors.

Ashton Rogers

WHY IS IT ALWAYS DOLLS?
A.W. PERRY HOMESTEAD MUSEUM

As someone who loves science and history, I spend a lot of my free time in museums when I have the chance. Local history museums are my favorite because the pieces stored within are significant to the area's history. Walking among the dusty artifacts and antiquity of the past gives me a real sense of connection. I've often imagined myself in the place of the people who built, used, and kept the items I was viewing from the other side of glass cases and velvet ropes. It's this process that has helped me understand people on a deeper level. Because people's belief is so firmly rooted to what they were taught by our ancestors, this connection is crucial to our field.

One of my favorite museums to have visited was the Jefferson Historical Museum in east Texas. It was the first time I had been in one of the small local history museums. I was intrigued by all the town history preserved there and truly enjoyed the experience. Later that night, I took the ghost tour and found out that there were reports of paranormal activity in the museum. Many people reported having seen a very realistic looking Native American mannequin on the top floor at the end of the hallway upon entering. However, when they got to the end of the hall they would find that it was not there. While I sadly didn't have that experience, the story fascinated me. There is a strongly held belief by people that spirits can be attached to not just places, but people and objects as well. By that logic, it makes sense that museums would be some of the best places for paranormal activity. And, it's that thought process that has made me obsessed with local history museums ever since.

So, when I received an email from the A.W. Perry Homestead Museum in Carrollton, Texas asking if we would meet with them, there was simply no way I could turn down the opportunity.

When we met with Victoria at the museum it was already after hours. She gave us a private tour and told us everything we could possibly want to know about the beautiful turn-of-the-century house and all the awesome pieces inside. The house was a white, American Colonial style house originally built by the A.W. Perry in 1857. In 1909, their son Dewitt Perry and his wife Francis tore down the first house and used some of the lumber to build the present-day house. After the family stopped using it as their home, it was remodeled in 1976 and turned into a museum. The house is a perfectly preserved example of life during the turn of the century, filled with furniture and personal belongings of the family as well as other pieces donated over time. We heard many stories about the family and their prominent role in the early days of Carrollton.

We would find that a few of the Perry children had passed away in the original house during the 1850's. In those days, two out of three kids never made it to maturity. A.W. and his wife Sara were laid to rest in the cemetery across the street from the museum, never far from home. And, Francis, who was the last relative to live in the home, passed there in the 1960's. She was well over a hundred years old. It was after her passing that the family would donate the property to the city.

Initially, we thought that we might get a chance to investigate the museum, but quickly found out that the head curator at the time was very opposed to the idea. The concern was that with so many valuable pieces inside, they did not want anything damaged. Not something the event's coordinator, Victoria, agreed with. But, understandable nonetheless. Instead we had been invited to participate in a presentation panel that the museum would be giving in October in preparation for Halloween with a few other groups. Always enjoying the opportunity to network and meet with people, we happily agreed.

Later, that October, the panel went very well. We were able to talk alongside two other local paranormal groups to several people and present our ideas and evidence. To our surprise, we were one of the more well-received groups that were presenting that day. Initially we had been nervous, still being a new group, but all hit our stride and relaxed a bit after answering a few questions. During the panel, as Victoria had predicted based on previous encounters with visitors, one of the crowd members asked if the house was haunted. Victoria shared some of the cool experiences she had in the past in the house just like she had with us. Of course, the next question to follow was if any of us had investigated the house yet. Before anyone could answer, one of the gentlemen who was on the panel with us interrupted.

"Not yet, but I will be soon." The answer confused me since I knew Victoria had expressly told all the investigative team's months before that there wouldn't be any investigations happening. But, glancing up at our host and seeing her annoyed expression, I immediately knew that he was just talking to hear himself speak. This guy had been rather arrogant and most of the other investigators had not been impressed with his pushy attitude. Eventually we wrapped up the panel, shook hands, and went home for the night.

Sometime in April of the next year, I was pleased to find an email in my inbox from Victoria wanting to know if we would be interested in returning in October for the second annual paranormal panel. Happy that we were liked enough to be invited back, I immediately accepted the invitation. Not thinking anything of it, I asked her if she there had been any more activity since the last time we spoke. I was overjoyed by her reply.

"...actually, we have had a few more things happen out of the ordinary. But, since you ask, we have a new curator now. Would you still be interested in coming out to do an investigation? - Victoria"

I didn't want to seem too eager, but I could not reply *yes* fast enough. I immediately got with the group to start checking our schedule for availability.

As it turned out, the gentleman who had seemed so pushy at the previous panel was exactly how he seemed. Apparently, he had continued to bother the staff about doing an investigation, enough that he wasn't even invited back for the next panel. Ultimately it was our policy of not being annoyingly persistent that paid off in getting us in the door. We were all very enthusiastic about the opportunity to investigate the house because it was advance enough notice that we knew we could produce a video of our findings in time for the panel. It also meant that our presentation could include findings specific to the location. Also, since the house had been built, we would be the first and only investigators to be allowed the opportunity.

Our investigation ended up taking place in July. Sara, Allie, and I all met with Victoria and her intern, John, at the house just before sundown. After unloading the car, I started our routine of taking reference photos inside and outside the house before I ran out of daylight, while our hosts gave Allie and Sara a refresher tour of the house. After I finished taking pictures, we conducted interviews with John and Victoria for the camera, in which they recounted the history of the house, family, and told us about their experiences.

Victoria would tell us about how she had several personal experiences in the house. Strange feelings of not being alone, electronic malfunctions such as Wi-Fi and cell service stopping and starting, strange sounds in the house like someone moving around, and strange smells were common. None of these were experiences that frightened her, but admittedly more curious than anything. She told us about some troubling times that she had gone through while working at the museum and felt like whatever was there was comforting her. She spent so much time at the homestead it was virtually her second home. She had become so accustomed to the activity she almost didn't notice it anymore and would often talk to the house itself on days she was there alone.

Victoria would not be the only one to have those experiences, as she would tell us. Several guests and volunteer staff would report much of the same things from time to time.

John's reports indicated that he had not only experienced some of the aforementioned activity for himself, but on one occasion when he was alone upstairs, he suddenly heard a crash. After checking to see what it was, found that a heavy box had been knocked down from a shelf prominently labeled "Doll Heads." After taking a step towards the box, he got a sinking feeling in his chest and decided that it was simply time to close the museum for the night. He would go on to tell us that sometimes, while prepping for tours or after one had completed, he would find indentions on the bed in the nursery room. Those indentions would remarkably look like someone had been sitting on the bed. This is not possible since the bed cannot support the weight of a person due to no supports being in the bed, which was just placed as an ornamental exhibit.

While some of the staff would have experiences to report, the majority did not. To them it was just an old house with old stuff in it. However, even for those who hadn't seen or heard anything from themselves, they would frequently voice their opinions of the creepy nature of the dolls placed in the nursery.

It's a well-known fact that dolls rose in popularity during the 1840's and it would not be uncommon for children, especially little girls, to own several dolls. The Perry family was no different, and would leave the lifelike reminders behind in the house as a testament to their legacy. Many of the dolls displayed in the nursery had very lifelike features, including painted eyes, detailed features, and even human hair on some. One baby doll, whose home was on the same bed that would sometimes have strange indentations, had a very happy and loving expression on its face, but in the right context it could make your skin crawl.

As a side note, Victoria told us, that the only case of theft had actually occurred in the nursery. Originally, they used to keep a doll sitting by the window in an antique bassinet. However, one day they came in to find that the doll was missing, and the window was broken. During the night someone had punched in the window and taken the doll. Likely kids, but she admitted she liked to tell people that the doll broke out on its own and was terrorizing people somewhere. Though the story was amusing, the thought did not sit well. As a joke, I asked to the other dolls in the room if they missed their friend. The silence was deafening.

Pediophobia is a well-documented psychological fear of dolls or similar objects. Ernst Jentsch theorized that uncanny feelings arise in the human mind when there is an intellectual uncertainty about whether an object is alive or not. Later, Freud would further develop the observation. More recently, Japanese roboticist Masahiro Mori expanded these theories to develop the *uncanny valley hypothesis*: if an object is obviously enough non-human, its human characteristics will stand out and be endearing; however, if that object reaches a certain threshold of human-like appearance, its non-human characteristics will stand out, and be disturbing.

Had I known at the time that one of our investigators, Kristin, suffered from the condition I would have made sure to schedule on a night that she could attend. I find it interesting to see how fears play into the perception of a paranormal investigation and how it changes the experience and results. Sadly though, I hadn't been aware, and she wasn't available that night.

Victoria told us a more detailed history about the location as we were digging in, looking for auxiliary information that could help us on the investigation. There were some deaths in the house, as to be expected with a house that had remained with a family for a little more than a century. We also learned that there had been a slave quarters on the property at some point, but it had been torn down during the original rebuild and it was no longer known where it had stood. Almost every stick of furniture in the building had its own story, a good portion of it being original to the house.

After taking baseline readings with an EMF detector around the house, we found there was really nothing of note. Poking around in the upstairs area, which is normally off limits to guests, I found my way to a door that led into the attic. Opening the door and peering inside, the room was pitch black. Pulling my phone from my pocket I switched on my flashlight app and looked around. I nearly fell backwards out of the door as my light came across the figure of a person standing in front of me, in what initially looked like 1800's clothing. Stumbling over myself and gaining my composure I looked again as I heard laughter coming from the main landing. John immediately began to apologize. He forgot to tell me that they had a mannequin stored behind the door. Taking a breath, I glanced around, the room felt eerie and chilled. The look of it reminded me of the final scene in The Conjuring where Elizabeth Warren had to climb through the walls. There were obvious signs that there were rodents living in the attic, which meant strange noises could be expected on quiet nights.

Eager to get started, Victoria killed the lights. This was the first time that the main lights had been shut off in the house with people inside at night. Even Victoria, who spent the most time of everyone at the location was now seeing the building in a new medium. We all paused for a moment to absorb the new feeling that the building had taken on.

"Let's get started." Sara said as she flipped on her digital recorder.

During our initial EVP sessions, Allie would take several photographs in multiple visual spectrums. In almost every single picture she would note that there was a high concentration of orbs that would surround group members as the ran their experiments. To debunk the idea that these orbs were paranormal, she switched over to using her array of Monowavelength light filters. In every photo the orbs would come back as the color of light that she was using, proving that the orbs that were being captured in our photos and video were just dust particles floating around in the air. We hadn't realized how dusty the museum was until we were looking at it under infrared light.

Not getting any responses that we could detect, in a group setting, we decided to let John start the first solo EVP session. In every noted case of paranormal experience with the house, the subject was always alone. So, we figured there might be some logic to having the subjects perform experiments on their own in case, our group, were elements causing paranormal activity not to happen. After some brief and specific instructions on the proper methods for conducting an EVP session, we left John alone in the house while we all went outside to occupy our time by the barn well out of sound contamination range.

It wasn't hard to occupy the group as, within minutes, they

spotted a raccoon hiding by a tree near the barn. The animal was surprisingly tame and let the girls come within feet of him to take pictures and baby talk him to his heart's content. Seeing as how the museum is surrounded by a city park, he was probably used to people feeding him. Observing the wildlife helped further confirm the theory that there were animals living in the attic that could be causing some of the strange noises that the staff would hear when it was quiet.

John was feeling a little uneasy being in the house alone for the first time with the lights off, so he ran through each room session quickly, only asking about four or five questions per room. We had also left him with the live-stream camera, so I was able to monitor his progress from the barn area on my cell phone. Eventually he found his way downstairs into the room made up as a nursery. After John settled into the corner and got still he began his questions. From the video it was obvious he was uncomfortable in the dark with all the antique dolls staring back at him from the shadows.

"Are there any spirits inhabiting our dolls?" he asked, probably hoping not to receive an answer. In the seconds that followed, a strange noise can be heard on the recording. In the background a sound that resembles someone getting up or sitting on the bed is followed by a soft whispering that sounds like a child. John didn't remember hearing it at the time, but in the video, he looks toward the bed as if he did. He may have subconsciously ignored the noise out of fear. When we checked the DVR footage, we verified that his body was not moving at the time the sound was produced. Sound analysis also showed that the whisper sound we captured was recorded at the 233 Hz range, which is well within normal parameters of human speech, however since we can see John is neither moving or talking we know that it was not him making this noise. To further affect, the group was outside well out of range of the house, so we know it was not sound contamination.

It was obvious that Jon was not a fan of the room from the DVR footage. Having a room full of porcelain dolls staring back at you is bad enough. Being told that you must stand in there perfectly still, in the dark, and talk to them is another matter entirely. I'm sure that he had envisioned one of the little figures moving several times and fought the urge to run. After only five questions John made his escape into the kitchen area. Thinking back on the investigation, I only wish that Kristen had been there to force into the room. Her fear of dolls, stemming back to her childhood experience, would have made for an interesting experiment.

Not knowing that he had captured evidence in the creepiest of rooms, John joined us out by the barn to let us know he was done. After reviewing the digital recorder, he was using, and hearing the strange sound, Victoria was eager to take a turn by herself. She has such a strong connection with the location that she was anxious to find out if there was anything there wanting to communicate with her. So, once again, we went over procedures and sent her inside while the rest of us waited out by the barn.

Starting in the same location as John, upstairs, Victoria would take a little longer to run her EVP sessions. Several of her questions were personal and emotionally connected to things that had gone on in the house. She talked about a breakup she had gone through while working there, friends she had brought there, and addressed specific members of the family whose stories she identified with. Taking great care and time in each room, eventually, she found her way into the parlor where she took a seat on the antique piano bench next to the piano she had played so many times before. After several other questions, eventually she asked:

"Why do you make us come downstairs?" This was referring to times that her and John would be working in the upstairs offices and suddenly hear voices and furniture moving on the first floor, only to find no trace of the source. While she didn't hear it at the time, playback of the recorder would reveal a very faint moaning sound in the background recorded in the 44 Hz frequency range. While this is in the normal range of hearing, it was missed at the time. It is of note that a sound in that range would probably not be produced by human vocal cords without considerable concentrated effort. Upon finding the evidence, we would later check the video footage to make sure that there was nothing we could spot making the noise. We looked for cars going by, checked the surrounding area for industrial equipment that could be causing the sound and found nothing. We are also reasonably certain that Pavarotti was not hiding in the couch cushion singing low F just to mess with us.

After wrapping up her solo EVP session Victoria came outside to retrieve us. When we re-entered the house, everyone gathered into the parlor to take a break. To pass the time, Sara played some period music from her phone as an attempt to trigger activity, and I went through DVR footage from the past couple of hours to see if I could catch a glimpse of anything unusual. While watching one of the replays, I almost jumped out of my seat when I saw a human shadow figure walk by the camera in the nursery room. Trying not to get too excited, I checked all the separate cameras to take stock of where everyone was at. Confident nobody was in the house when it happened, I started to go through outside footage. That's when my heart sank. Looking at the outside shot of the building, it was obvious that the shadow was caused by myself walking by the window earlier. Disappointed, I finished reviewing the footage and went on to join the group, who had just turned off the period music.

After sitting in silence for a while, with nothing happening, we decided to try using an SB-7 Spirit Box to see if we got anything unusual. Since the last time I had used the device, I had made a slight modification to it by removing the antenna. The hope was that it would cut down on the amount of radio interference that I would receive from legitimate transmissions. I hadn't tested it out yet, so I was curious what the result would be. After letting it sweep through several stations on the FM band, I found that even without an antenna attached to it, FM stations came in loud and clear. Trying the AM band, I got the same results. It was clear that the only way I would be able to filter out radio wave interference would be to construct a faraday cage for the device. Something I would have to save for another investigation. However, not all was lost for the experiment.

Even though none of the voices we received could be verified, we still let the unit run. It's thought that the static white noise can help build energy in the area for entities to use. Using this logic, we decided that we would go ahead and try to ask questions and see if anything came through in the channels we knew were dead, just for the sake of trying, even though we knew none of the results could be validated. Nothing came through that was relevant to our questions or didn't sound like a brief segment of radio station transmission. However, when running part of the session upstairs, Allie and I noticed several places in the house where the transmission would be interrupted. We were able to verify with an EMF detector that there were parts of the house that acted as a natural faraday cage and would block signal. We noted this as a possible reason for some of the reported electronic malfunctions in the house. It's possible something about the construction of the house interferes with wireless devices and radios.

As we were winding down for the night, most of us had gathered in the parlor and were discussing past cases. Like many times on our investigations, we will take breaks from experimenting just to socialize. Not only does it help relieve the tension of a long night, but we feel that the socialization might encourage activity. On many cases we find that some of the best evidence is found when we aren't looking for it, but rather like something is trying to interact with us while we are focused elsewhere. During our conversation, Sara began to feel like we were being watched from the other room across the main hallway. It's really the first time any of my team members have felt strange since being in the house, so we all quieted down while she took a camera to go look.

Creeping slowly and softly into the room while the rest of us held our breath, Sara began to film a section of house across the hall. As she entered the main living room across from the parlor, a strange whispering voice was captured on her video recorder. At the time she was also carrying a live high-sensitivity digital recorder that we would find did not capture the noise. Reviewing footage of the static DVR's, we can see that the noise was not one of the investigator's voices. Since the video recorder is the only unit to pick up the sounds, we were able to conclude that it originated in close proximity to the camera's microphone, but was too quiet to be heard by the other device that Sara was wearing. Analysis of the sound showed that it was produced in the 28 Hz range which is at the bottom of human hearing, and below what human vocal cords can normally produce.

The rest of the night passed by relatively uneventfully. Walking the grounds outside, I only captured sound contamination and the accusing eyes of our racoon friend in my camera. Not knowing where the slave quarters were located, and not being led there by any guiding spirits, did not make for anything exciting. Sadly, at the time of my investigation, we never thought to ask to check out the graveyard across the street. However, I was assured by Victoria later that we could come back to do a follow-up and we would have access to the cemetery as well.

As we packed up for the night, I was rather thankful to have the lights back on before going into the nursery. Even though I had not captured any evidence in there myself, just having seen it secondhand gave me chills. Looking at the tiny faces of those porcelain dolls somehow did not sit right with me. Later, when talking to Victoria, she admitted that she always made a point to be pleasant to the dolls out of fear that they might come to life and come after her one day. As amusing as it sounds, staring into their eyes does unsettle a person.

The museum had a deep and rich history that was easy to let ourselves become entwined with. Sitting among all the antiquity and taking it all in was haunting. Museums have a different feeling once all the people leave, the lights are out, and the noise from the world is just a distant echo. I didn't think I could love a museum any more than I already do, but then I discovered a whole new side to it. Museums are living and breathing pieces of history, not dead time capsules just to be viewed from the other side of a piece of glass. I think I understand the connection now that Victoria had described. Having spent so much time there, working and caring for the place, it has become her home. Like many of those pieces, she has also become a permanent fixture within its walls. I'm grateful for her invitation.

A few months after our investigation we would present our findings at the second panel, which was even bigger than the first. Afterwards, Victoria played the teaser for our video on the side of the barn, followed by the original *House on Haunted Hill*. The event really took off and is now an annual event that I hope to participate in for the foreseeable future. Since the popularity of the investigation, the museum also now runs evening tours in October.

Should you ever find yourself in Carrollton, Texas with some time to spare, stop by the A.W. Perry Homestead Museum and see it for yourself. Just be sure to be nice to the dolls.

Ashton Rogers

LEAVING THE GATE OPEN
KYLE CEMETERY AND HAMM CREEK
Sara Hatfield

Since the beginning, when I first started hunting ghosts on my own, I just wanted to find something that would change the way I perceived the world around me. I wanted answers. After, Ashton had his experience and decided to pour his spare time, money, and knowledge into the hobby I loved so much, I used it as a mutual vehicle to bring me closer to that goal. Only now, as part of a team, with a budget to do the experiments I always wanted to try. It was my goal to revisit all the interesting places I had fallen in love with over the years to see if the things I had experienced in my life were just in my head, or if there was something real to be found by pulling back the curtain. Sometimes though, the answers to those questions might surprise you, rearrange your insides, and scare the hell out of you for reasons you can't even explain even with the evidence right in front of you.

I wish I could say that our first trip to Kyle was a surreal and visceral experience. But, like most things, the truth is that it was hardly even noteworthy at the time. Initially I found Kyle Cemetery by accident when I was sixteen. I found it tucked away, hidden at the end of a random unmarked dirt trail that jutted off one of my favorite roads to speed down with the radio blasting, County Road 916.

The cemetery itself is a square and fenced in with a chain link style enclosure. The whole thing is surrounded by thick trees on three sides. The only clearing being the cemetery itself and the entrance area which is just a rough gravel lot for cars to park which abruptly cuts into denser wooded area. One of the things I love so much about the location was the half dozen or so trees inside the cemetery that stood twisted and broken from years of harsh Texas storms. All monuments to the lonely forgotten nature of the location.

The night of our initial scouting trip to the cemetery was so uneventful and calm, that the only reason we even bothered to go back there was because we thought it would be a good location to shoot a video about debunking common mistakes made by other investigators. The cemetery was a million miles away from anything, completely enclosed, dark, and void of anything even remotely paranormal. There were no stories or rumors that we knew about and best of all no interruptions. We spent about an hour there that first night walking the property, the cemetery seemed huge, old and full of character. In the back were the remains of a fence near a dilapidated wooden structure that used to be an outdoor bathroom. Beyond the fence was a long straight path about arm's length wide beautifully canopied by tall broadleaf trees. I can remember us joking that it was the path that took you beyond the graveyard into the *pet cemetery,* a reference to one of my favorite stories by Stephen King. I explored the path walking it for about sixty yards before I suddenly realized I had left the group behind and decided I should rejoin them. Disappointed I didn't get to see where the path led, nor did I encounter a creepy person telling me that *the land was sour,* I quickly joined them near the back fence where we finished our scouting. We wouldn't return to shoot our video until two weeks later when everyone's schedules would allow for it.

It was late November in 2015 when we started filming our first "official" investigation at Kyle. We really had no idea, at the time, that it would become an ongoing case that would last three years. It just seemed that no matter how much we thought we were done with the place, we would always find that it would not be done with us.

As soon as the cameras began rolling things just seemed to immediately fall apart. We used every bit of our experience we had up to that point to try and figure out what was happening, but to no avail. In the first section, located by the more densely populated part of the cemetery, we would begin to hear footsteps in the darkness. This is something we all heard at the time and reacted to, but no amount of checking would ever reveal the source. Thinking that it could be animals we spent a fair amount of time sitting still and watching through the thermal camera but could never pinpoint a source. At one point I would ask *Is there anything that would like to communicate with us.* And, while it wasn't heard by any of us at the time, the distant sound of crying could be heard on our analog tape recorder upon review. Because we were filming at the time, we were easily able to rule out that any of us were making the noise.

Sometime later, as we were getting ready to change positions in the cemetery, we were all startled when Ashton suddenly started scrambling backwards to get away from the back fence and shouting excitedly. While Allie and I had been finishing up some readings in our location, he had moved up ahead with his sister to get setup for the next spot. While doing so, he heard a very loud and distinct growling noise right in front of him. His initial instincts didn't tell him that there was a malevolent spirit trying to get him, but a hungry animal warding him off. Kady, who had also heard the noise, had been filming the exact spot with a thermal camera the whole time and continued to scan the area after. While Ashton was dead sure that there was a dog or coyote just feet away from him, Kady found nothing on the video. It was several minutes before he was able to collect himself enough to even physically go back to the area.

Almost on cue, as he did, at the level of a loud whisper, we all heard it. The sounds of an animal in pain. Like bait on a hook, Allie and I instinctively tried to locate the missing, hurt, pup that we just had to rescue. After a long time of looking using the thermal camera, flashlights, IR lights, and everything else in our bag of tricks, the men's voices that we had been ignoring finally began to pierce into our heads. We had temporarily lost our minds trying to find this animal and the whole time the guys had been telling us what a bad idea it was. Not only would we inherently anger whatever animal had growled at Ashton when we found it, it might attack us. Not only that, with our equipment, if there was actually an animal we would have found it by then. The guys had a bad feeling that we were being corralled like lambs to a slaughter, and Justin was already beginning to throw out the idea of leaving. And just like that, as suddenly as it had come on it went away. As if the realization that there could potentially not be an actual animal there triggered it, the sounds stopped all together.

Frustrated with us ignoring his warnings and refusing to leave, Justin posted up in the car to watch the static cameras while we ventured further in to continue with the investigation. For about fifteen minutes as a group we conducted some simple EVP's and readings by a child's grave, getting nothing, when Justin's voice crackled in over the walkie-talkie. He told us he just saw something walk across the shot at the back-fence line that he couldn't identify and that we should probably back off. Ignoring the warning, we all moved forward towards the back-gate area. Almost, as if in a waking dream state, it seemed like even if I tried to move with the group I would somehow end up separated by great distances. As if I was just wandering off into the night. Even though I was being deliberate about my movements, somehow spatial reasoning just went out the window. Slowly we moved toward the back gate and immediately froze in our tracks when we saw what waited for us there. We all saw something together that would stick with us the rest of our lives.

Silently we stared into the darkness filming unable to move and unsure of what had just happened. I saw something horrible that gives me such an uneasy feeling to this day. It passed from right to left across the gap in the fence in what must have been just a few moments, but my brain slowed the scene down like it does when an emergency happens. It felt like I had a long time to stare at whatever it was, but it was so encased in shadow that it was hard to see much of it. Much less, process what was happening.

I saw what, at first, I thought was a very tall man, almost seven feet. Most of him was barely a shadow, an outline at best. His legs immediately stood out to me and kept my attention for the duration of the incident. They were very long, bulky, and wrong. My mind wouldn't accept what I was seeing, and it just kept telling me that they were WRONG like an alarm going off in my head. It took a lot of pondering before I figured out most of what bothered me about the legs. It was as if they had an extra joint, or perhaps the knee was backward. Almost as if a four-legged animal had been trying to walk on its back legs. While that still doesn't describe it well enough, I'm not sure I'll ever comprehend exactly what was WRONG with those legs. Yet, it stood up straight. Too straight. An animal such as a bear walking on its back legs still leans forward and hunches. An animal doesn't have the upright posture of a human that is primarily bipedal.

We all saw a part of it at the exact same time, but couldn't say anything just frozen. We all felt it without communicating. We stood there for nearly a minute before Ashton was the first to break the silence.

I saw what, at first, I thought was a very tall man, almost seven feet. Most of him was barely a shadow, an outline at best. His legs immediately stood out to me and kept my attention for the duration of the incident. They were very long, bulky, and wrong. My mind wouldn't accept what I was seeing, and it just kept telling me that they were WRONG like an alarm going off in my head. It took a lot of pondering before I figured out most of what bothered me about the legs. It was as if they had an extra joint, or perhaps the knee was backward. Almost as if a four-legged animal had been trying to walk on its back legs. While that still doesn't describe it well enough, I'm not sure I'll ever comprehend exactly what was WRONG with those legs. Yet, it stood up straight. Too straight. An animal such as a bear walking on its back legs still leans forward and hunches. An animal doesn't have the upright posture of a human that is primarily bipedal.

We all saw a part of it at the exact same time, but couldn't say anything just frozen. We all felt it without communicating. We stood there for nearly a minute before Ashton was the first to break the silence.

"I kind of don't want to say what I just saw and influence you guys... I don't know if my eyes are playing tricks on me. But, I swear I just saw something walk by the fence from right to left. It was very tall." As soon as the words left his mouth my heart nearly stopped. Could he really have just seen what I saw? He continued on "It was like a person, but tall. Like, seven feet tall; with a coat or something weird like strafed from the right side of the fence over to the left. Like it was walking, but it wasn't normal. Like it was moving sideways or something." I wanted to respond buy I felt like I was in shock. Finally, I was able to whisper over to Allie.

"Its legs weren't right. They were wrong." Ashton didn't hear me say it, but Allie just turned and looked at me and I could see that she knew I was being serious. Ashton and I began to back away, we all sensed that it was time to wrap things up. As we were beginning our slow retreat Allie called out to us.

"I just saw a face poking out at us." We all suddenly paused and looked where Allie was pointing. I couldn't move. "Right there, it like stuck it's head out and looked at us. It was high up like it was checking us out."

Ashton and I both asked her what it looked like. At the time she only described it as a white face. But, later that night, after we had left she would recount it with far more detail as a human shaped face, painted chalk white with thick cracking lead paint. The hair was black and greasy and the eyes sunken in and solid black. Most notably the place she saw it peeking out was just above the rear gate fence post which sits at exactly seven and a quarter foot tall.

Normally we wait a few days before going over evidence, but when we back to my house that night we immediately started going through footage, pictures, and audio from the investigation. Specifically, we looked at all the video from that section of the location and particularly around the time of the event. While we were able to document the experience fully, there was no evidence that we could point to definitively to corroborate what we all saw. It was nearly 5:00 AM and we needed to sleep. The team slept over at my place and we decided that we would get up the next day to check the place out in the daylight. We reasoned that if there had been an animal out there we would be able to maybe find some tracks in the woods on the other side of the fence. We weren't positive we'd find answers, but we needed to do something. None of us slept well and I know I wasn't the only one to have nightmares.

Returning in the daytime didn't feel the same at all. The negativity was gone, but what we found will haunt me personally for the rest of my life. Pulling up to the front gate we immediately felt like something was off, but we just couldn't place it. Everything looked entirely different. After about ten minutes of walking around we realized that the cemetery was only about half the size that we had all remembered. Everything was where it should be relative to each other, but the whole place just seemed compressed somehow. It was strange, but we all assumed it was just our spatial reasoning being messed up from wandering around in the dark. However, once we exited out the back gate to look at the trail on the other side, I felt like I had lost my mind entirely.

As we stepped through the gate we immediately realized that there was no trail at all. No tall trees, no trail, not even a wooded area. What had been this long thick wooded and canopied trail was now almost a completely open field with only a handful of trees dispersed along the fence line. Standing here we, all said the same thing out loud to each other. *This was not like this before.* We argued for an hour about how we could have mistaken this back lot as a wooded area, but nothing we came up with really fit. Furthermore, I had walked back into this section before we ever started filming. It was a long straight trail that I had distinctly remembered walking down.

We spent the rest of the time looking for any evidence that animals had been out there the night before and even though the dirt was soft and easily showed tracks we could find nothing. No tracks, no dens, and no dropping. We were also able to note that the trees by the fence were so sparse that if an animal had been there the most definitely would have shown up on the thermal camera. Frustrated and stunned we packed up and left very confused about everything that we had experienced. Over the course of the next month, we did research on the area to see if there was any background we didn't know about. We would never have guessed what he uncovered.

In our downtime, Ashton researched the location the location while I did some checking of my own. The changing of the landscape and the strange thing that we all saw struck and unsettling chord in me. I had never heard of anything like that happening in real life and I wanted to know if anyone else had experienced the same. My searches ranged from strange articles about the Mandela Effect to bigfoot. One thing stood out to me, and that was an article I read about the *Navajo Skinwalkers*. These were creatures that could distort space and time, imitate other voices, and existed as either a goat-man hybrid or coyote. As farfetched as it sounded, some of the stories I read about these creatures eerily echoed some of the events of our investigation.

In Ashton's side of the research, he never found any direct stories about the cemetery being *haunted*. However, an internet search for the area of Hamm Creek and Rio Vista did reveal several accounts of haunted roads and spectral hitchhikers, as well as, several claims of poltergeist activity in the houses along those same roads. It was while going down that rabbit hole that he discovered that the back roads of Rio Vista were more than they seemed.

Since as far back as the 1960s, the community of Rio Vista has maintained a high missing persons rate. Johnson county is notorious for people gone missing and bodies being found. This is of significance since the town of Rio Vista's main urban legend is that of a spectral female hitchhiker, with no shoes, and often no face. She is believed to be the spirit of one of these missing persons; possibly one of the unnamed victims of a local serial killer, Kenneth McDuff, who was thought to be active between

1966 through 1992 with accomplice Roy Green. Several cold cases remain open in the area involving violent crimes and missing persons, almost any of which could explain the specter. Because of the seclusion of the area, it's no surprise that it is an easy place for criminals to hide their sinister evidence. The Johnson County Sheriff we talked with has made great strides in solving many of these cold cases bringing seven of the most troubling to conclusion.

As far as our research could tell, the story of the hitchhiker has legitimate roots going back to the mid 1970's. Some locals claiming that it's the spirit of a girl that went missing in the late 60's. However, nobody seems to remember who that person was as is the case when trying to pin down most of these urban legends. But, as interesting as those stories were, they had little bearing on the experiences we had. Although the rest of us had given up trying to find anything related to our investigation, Ashton kept digging and eventually found a very startling answer in the history of the town.

In 1801, long before Texas independence, after several trips into the area of the Sabine River to capture wild horses; Horse-Trader Phillip Nolan advanced inland with a party of eighteen men as far as the Brazos River. At nightfall the party was attacked by the natives, and Nolan was killed. The nearby river was eventually named after him. The Nolan river runs directly through and joins with Hamm Creek being an offshoot that would become a route that horse traders and thieves would use to guide them through the area. It's also of note that this directly connects to another area of local legend known as "Old Foamy" which is famous for its Goatman stories.

The Anadarko Indians under the leadership of chief Jose Maria, occupied the Hamm Creek area during the 1830s and discouraged any kind of settlement due to it being considered a sacred land. Today several areas within and surrounding it are thought to be sacred sites possibly used for burial by the Anadarko and Caddo at one time or another. *It's this exact area geographically that we would find that we had been conducting our investigation.*

Eventually, the Anadarko were convinced to the make peace in 1849 when Henry Briden, his wife came into the area. At the Nolan River west of Rio Vista, they found springs of water and constructed a log cabin, which would be considered the first house in Johnson County. Soon after more white men wanted to settle the area but were still met with some resistance. However, five miles west of Nolan River, near Hamm Creek, of what is now considered Rio Vista the settlers eventually banded with the Anadarko to help drive out the Comanche to gain their favor. Once again, we found significance in the area we had been investigating. It was in that spot, on that sacred land, a skirmish took place that left 75 Comanche dead, and unknown wounded.

Because the Comanche were considered so bad to the Anadarko. They scalped and denied any Comanche proper burials for their culture. Apparently, the white settlers were not happy about the bodies that the Anadarko left behind and had refused to move. The settlers would eventually go back on their deal and force the Anadarko off their land to move into the Oklahoma territory. Obviously, the Anadarko not happy about the betrayal cursed the area with the summoning of a *skinwalker* to protect their burial lands. They told the white man they could have the land, but that it would endure terrible hardships until it was returned to its rightful people.

The community that was built in place of the Anadarko area was originally known as Grange Hall and Kimbell before 1881, when the Gulf, Colorado and Santa Fe Railway was completed a mile east and the townsite of Rio Vista was laid out overlooking the Nolan River and Mustang Creek. Grange Hall declined, and Rio Vista grew. In 1884 residents from neighboring Derden, Nathan, Hart, and Sullivan moved to the new site and eventually our little area nestled within Hamm Creek would get tucked away in a back road and forgotten by all, until I managed to stumble across it by chance.

The history that we found was sad and all too familiar to anyone familiar with Texas history. But, what was significant was that the geographical location seemed to be the epicenter of a lot of historical information that seemed to indicate that maybe we weren't just going insane. Not only was the area considered sacred ground that had had seen its share of violence, it was the location of a legitimate curse involving a skinwalker of all things. Upon hearing this, and having just researched this very myth, things began to become just a little too real.

Skinwalkers, sometimes referred to as "Goat Men", are a well-known (but rarely talked about) legends mainly associated with the Navajo. However, other tribes also had their own versions and takes of the same creature in their culture and stories. It's believed that the skinwalker is a witch or creature that can change its shape and voice to try to mimic people. Sometimes the creature is described as a protector, while other sources claim that it is a Native American with that has been corrupted by their magic. The skinwalkers true form is always something that doesn't appear as human, usually a goat or coyote human hybrid. The creature can change shape to blend in as part of your group to try to get closer to you. It can even mimic human voices, although something always seems to sound off about them.

Of course, with most legends there were conflicting stories and facts. But, the more we studied it was the littler things that would stand out. The entire time we had been at Kyle it felt like we were constantly being lured into a trap and watched from the shadows. The EVP's that we recorded sounded like a human voice, but something never quite fit about it in the scheme of what we were doing. The more we looked at this strange information, the more it just seemed like there was something to it.

It was shortly after we were starting to piece together the video from our first investigation when I had a chance conversation with my brother-in-law Jonathan who had also been to the property a few years earlier with some friends. Before I could even get into the strangeness of the story and explain what I saw he interrupted me with the strangest question. *What did its legs look like?* To this point I hadn't said anything about it other than it was tall. I couldn't believe what he had just said to me. Come to find out, some friends of his had seen something out there and had described seeing a creature with legs that almost looked backwards. He also went on to tell me that while driving down County Road 916 at a spot not far from Hamm Creek he had seen a strange, long and unnatural, white arm reaching out toward him from behind a large boulder that was on the side of the road. When he slowed down to take a closer look it disappeared. He never knew what to make of it but had found it strange. I immediately thought of Allie's description of the white face and knew that we would eventually have to go back to the location to investigate again.

We eventually went back in early April of 2016. After a lot of convincing, I finally got Ashton to agree to go back. Initially he was against the idea because at the time it was one of the few places he was legitimately concerned about not being safe for investigation. It was the first investigation we had conducted where anything negative had happened and it did not sit well with him. The tension in the car was thick as we pulled up to the gate. It had been a while since we had officially been back, and it felt like we all needed to calm down a little bit before we got started. But, once we got inside the fence the mood changed.

By this time, we had worked on several other cases and had a better feel for what we were doing as a team. The tension eased up and we all seemed to realize the location didn't have the same kind of feeling it did the first time we had investigated. For one, it felt smaller than it did before. It didn't have the grand feeling it had when we had previously been here at night. For our first experiments we used our flashlights and floods to see if we could figure out why the backlot would look like thick forest. But, nothing we did would create the illusion. It was easily visible that the back side of the fence was open with just a thin line of trees. There's no way that this was even close to what we had seen the previous time.

Just as we began to feel comfortable, thinking we were safe and nothing was going to happen, Allie heard footsteps. All of us standing about ten feet apart heard the same thing, footsteps sounding off in the middle of the cemetery between us. We could all clearly see the location that the sound was coming from and saw nothing. Ashton noted that there was nothing showing up on the thermal camera. That's when I suddenly realized, our attention had been drawn away from everything we had been doing. Just like that we had all turned our back on the entirety of the graveyard and nobody was looking. I felt like a cornered animal and it took everything inside me not to panic and calmly point out what I thought was plainly obvious.

Regrouping, we went through our routine of experiments eventually ending up again at the back gate. While taking a reading, Ashton hears what he thinks sounds like very quiet crying. Cautiously he leaned in toward the area that he thought he heard it coming from. As we all listened intently trying to hear what he has described, we became startled when we heard a small object like a rock hitting metal. The sound was captured very audibly on our recorders and we could easily tell that something had moved by the dilapidated remains of the bathroom. Most significantly though, when we watched the recording, strange arcs of light could be seen just on the other side of the fence where the sound had originated. However, we know in that direction there is nothing but trees and nothing for at least a mile that could even cause a light.

To this day I can't explain why, but even though we were all startled, Ashton decided to step through the gate at that moment and ask a question. As he did, he suddenly cut off what he was saying and asks. *Did you just say stop?* We all shook our heads as he turned to look at us, since none of us had said a word. I was worried about him being on the other side of the gate. I was just imagining something emerging from the woods, grabbing him and disappearing into the darkness. He re-addressed the question to the darkness.

"I won't go any further. Did you say stop? If you did say it again and we'll pack up and go." We all waited several seconds with baited breath. We didn't get a response. But, Ashton looked me in the eye and said. "I fucking heard *something* say stop when I was back there, and it didn't sound human. I want to go now." Within 10 minutes we were packing up our gear and heading home.

After that investigation I would never feel satisfied that we had debunked or proven anything. I decided that we should not only go back again, but several more times to see if multiple trips over the course of a long period of time would change our results. I wanted to know if we were just scaring ourselves or if there was really something out there. Ashton had reservations about going until I asked him a simple question. *If he had the chance to go back to the warehouse he had his first experience at to really collect evidence, would he do it?* By the end of the night we decided that I would be the lead investigator for the ongoing Kyle case and we started planning more trips and new experiments to try.

We would quickly find that we would capture the most evidence under two conditions: When we least expected to find anything, and when we were not at the location in full force. Although, we had been back two more times as a group we wouldn't find much of anything. Possible EVPs that were interesting, but ultimately be explained as contamination and a few orbs here and there which we were really starting to discredit almost entirely in our ongoing research. In August, that same year, Ashton called me to tell me that he had developed a new camera that he wanted to try out. It was based off one of our bigger rigs, but this one was smaller and had a wider field of view. The other interesting feature was that it could track objects further away while filming in the dark. Needing to bench test the unit, we took a short road trip to visit some places that we were acquainted with in the area. For no real reason at all I decided to take us down County Road 916 to cut back towards home. Ashton recognizing where we were suggested that we stop in at Kyle. Something that seemed a bit out of character for him considering his history with the location. Not one to argue about going to my favorite investigation spot, within ten minutes we were pulling up to the front gate. As the headlights pan over the cemetery Ashton slammed onto the brakes and shouts

"Did you see it!" and begins to point out the window and turns on his high-beams. Not having seen anything I almost hesitate to ask him what he was talking about. "I saw it. I swear I just saw it." I knew what he was talking about, but I was afraid to hear what would come out of his mouth. "I saw the thing. It was tall, and it was lanky. Like it was backwards. Like it was running backwards and ran out of the light." Suddenly I wanted to be anywhere but where we were. I told Ashton that we should leave and that this was a bad idea, but something was different.

By this time, I had probably been on at least twenty investigations with our lead. It was very clear from the start that he would never ask us to do anything we were truly uncomfortable with or scared to do. If something was too much, to this point, he would have been the first to offer to leave. But, this night something seemed wrong. The minute we had pulled up to the gates his entire demeanor had changed. When I asked him to leave he calmly told me *no*. At his suggestion we sat in the car for several minutes to calm down before going in, and even though I didn't want to for the first time in my life, I followed him into the gate.

Even with the camera in hand neither one of us could see to the back fence that now was dense with trees and a looming presence that made me feel like I may never get out of this place. We walked forward slowly into the abyss of the graveyard trying to see when the back would finally reveal itself like it always had in the past. Suddenly, it began as it always does, we hear footsteps just behind us, only this time, Ashton says that he hears someone saying something. As I turn to look, I hear a loud distinct voice from the darkness just feet from where we are standing. Panicked, I move closer to Ashton and tell him what I just heard. Laughing at me, Ashton continues to film my reactions as I gather up enough composure to start a quick EVP session even though I was physically shaking from the anxiety.

After only five questions I turn to Ashton to ask him once again if we can leave. As I do so, I spot what appears to be a large shadow in my flashlight in front of me. For a split second I really didn't think much of it, I thought I had just caught one of our shadows in the light. But, suddenly the realization hit me that the light was in front of us. The shadow was literally of something standing there blocking the light, and it was right in front of me. The next few seconds were a blur as my flight response took over. Screaming I knocked the camera from Ashton's hand into the darkness and ran in a full sprint back to the car where I jumped inside. Several moments later Ashton followed. It had taken him extra time because I had knocked his only light source into the darkness and he had to feel around blindly in the cemetery alone to find it. As he tried to get into the car I suddenly heard him frantically screaming obscenities at me from outside. I suddenly realized I had accidentally locked the door when I got in and he was trapped outside.

As soon as the doors were unlocked Ashton jumped into the car and relocked the door. He was almost in tears. He didn't look the same as he did just moments earlier as if the spell had worn off. We were both panicked and freaking out. After he caught his breath I began to bombard him with questions.

"How do we know each other, and what's the first investigation we did together?" Ashton looked confused. I repeated the questions. As he answered, the realization of what I was doing slowly dawned on him. I was testing him to make sure it was really him and not the *Goat-Man* pretending to be him. It seemed stupid, but I had to be sure. It was from that moment on we lightened up a little bit and started a long-standing tradition of quizzing each other before leaving Kyle.

We drove home and immediately watched the footage. While we didn't capture anything on video, the audio we captured was crystal clear. At the seconds between Ashton saying he heard something and me saying I just heard a voice, we in fact, captured a clear recording of what we both heard. Almost as if someone was doing an impression of my voice, *"I'm behind you"* can be clearly heard. However, not only am I in the shot not talking, I'm *in front* of Ashton at the time this is said.

To this day Ashton does not know where his aggressive nature came from that night. To make matters more unsettling, he admits to having trouble remembering how he found the camera I knocked out of his hand in the dark. To the best of his memory, I screamed, and he ran back to the car with me only to get locked out. However, because the equipment was running the whole time we can account for the exact timeline of everything. He also said that he had a bad bout of depression for about two weeks after the incident. It was because of this that we all started to wonder if not only was there a paranormal presence at Kyle, but was it somehow affecting us personally?

I wasn't even a full thirty days before we repeated the exact same process. In early September once again, we had new equipment to test. This time it was a camera and audio recording system that was wearable and hands free. After testing it out in another cemetery, I suggested we return to Kyle. Initially Ashton was not in favor of returning, but it didn't take much convincing to get him on board. By this time, we had all admitted we were addicted to finding out what was going on with this location.

When we got there, it took a good fifteen minutes to get the new equipment set up. That was unnerving, because without equipment in front of us to look at it felt like we were essentially blind. Finally, after an eternity of adjusting we were able to get started. We eschewed our normal routine and walked straight towards the middle of the graveyard. We began to relax as we noted that we could see through the trees, the moon was shining bright, and everything seemed still and quiet. These were the kind of nights at Kyle when we would get no activity which caused us to let our guard down. Ashton using the thermal camera, wandered out from my position about thirty yards, which made me a little nervous. Thinking back to our first nights here we had decided that separate was generally a bad idea. I called over to him to remind him and he looked confused. He hadn't realized that he had wandered so far away. Almost as soon as the realization hit him about what had happened his attention became split by a noise that was growing louder behind him in the darkness. It was the distinct sound of what I can only describe as animal hooves on hard dirt, like a horse at a full charge. He turned his head once, then back again and ran at me in a full sprint. At first, I thought he was just trying to get away until I realized he was trying to put himself in between whatever it was and myself. Ashton, pushing both of us out of the line of what we couldn't see pivoted us around and pointed the thermal camera at the sound that was still going.

"Do you hear it?" Ashton almost shouted at me as I tried to shush him. In fact, I did. Neither one of us had the thought that it was anything paranormal. Our first thought was that there was a wild animal loose in the cemetery about to attack us. But, no sooner did we turn to look did the sound just completely fade out of existence. Using both cameras we looked for the source for several minutes before we returned to the car. Ashton seemed frustrated and was cursing, at one point I thought he was laughing but I realized he was teared up. It was obvious that what had happened really affected him just now. After some coaching we got back to the car and I suggested that we call it a night. However, he had other plans.

"No, I'm tired of this thing chasing me out of here. We're doing an EVP session." He wasn't being pushy or out of character this time, just determined not to let us get pushed around by whatever this was. Unlike last time, I was excited to go back in and investigate.

Now each armed with a camera and a digital recorder we walked back in. This time we deliberately broke our own rule to see if it would illicit activity. I stayed by the front gate while Ashton walked back to the place we had just been ambushed to look for signs of tracks in the dirt. After a few minutes I began to get nervous and I called over for him to come back.

"Calm down." His tone was very sarcastic, and it sounded a bit off. But, it's not unusual for us to try to antagonize each other from time to time.

"Okay, sure." I replied nervously. Immediately I saw him turn towards me and ask

"Did you say something?" At first, I thought he was being a smartass, but as he walked back towards me I realized that he was genuinely asking. The exchange was a bit confusing because I was replying to what he said. I didn't think much of it at the time. However, when we went over the footage later we made a startling discovery. By syncing the recorders and video we were able to track our entire conversations over the course of the night. Disturbingly, we found some inconsistencies to say the least.

Replaying the sound of the hooves charging at us was startling enough, but it was Kristin who identified the EVP that immediately followed. After listening to the audio several times with headphones and boosting the audio we identified a section of audio that seemed to give us a very clear warning. *There's a monster in the woods.* A thought that had gone through all of our heads at one time or another now said plainly by God knows what.

We also found that a handful of times during the night it seemed that we would find ourselves replying to things the other had said. And, while those phrases were caught on our own recorders, it seemed they would be absent from the audio in the other. In the instance of Ashton walking away from me: On my recorder I can be heard telling him he should come back and his reply of *calm down,* as well as, everything after that. However, *his* recorder painted a different picture. When playing back the audio from the other device I can be heard in the distance asking him to come back. However, not having heard me say it himself, he didn't respond. *Calm down* is never said or recorded on the device that he is holding, an event that should be an impossibility. Upon realizing this, Ashton went back through all our audio on this and all previous investigations to find several instances of the same phenomenon. It became very apparent that something there had the ability to imitate our voices and my thoughts returned once again to the skinwalker legends.

With this new information we decided that we would change our tactics to focus on the audio phenomenon. We wanted to specifically capture the event on video. We decided that we would each carry digital recorders and a camera that we would keep pointed at ourselves to account for any talking that we did ourselves. The stakes were high, and we did not want to take any chances that our evidence would be called out as *audio contamination*.

It was late October when we finally went back. Typically, a month that we take off of investigations due to the fact that we're usually booked for panels and most places worth investigating are packed with teenagers trying to scare themselves for Halloween. However, having a free weekend and knowing that Kyle was not a well-known place, we felt that we could probably get an investigation in without any interruptions. As we pulled into the lot, Kristin began to get excited. This was the first time we had taken her on an investigation and we were going to test her skills as our new camera tech. Since we were starting to get more cases and use more equipment, Ashton had started becoming overloaded with things to do during prep time. This trip was going to serve as her trial by fire.

We were less than ten minutes into our setup when out of nowhere the car alarm began to go off. Thinking he had just accidentally hit the panic button, Ashton deactivated it. With a minute it started to go off again. This time, Ashton deliberately deactivated it and set his keys down on a headstone out of his pocket as to not set it off again. After another minute our activity was once again interrupted by the alarm sounding. Checking, we found that they keys had not moved. Knowing that Ashton had deactivated alarm, we all thought that it might be malfunctioning. Deactivating it again, we all headed over to the car to see if maybe there was something over there causing it to go off.

Checking out the area we could find no cause and stood around for several minutes waiting to see if it would happen again. When nothing happened, we decided to try an experiment. Holding the keys out visible to everyone, I began to ask some questions. On the third one we began to get activity.

"Do you want us to leave?" The alarm didn't sound, but the running lights on the car suddenly flashed making us jump. Ashton opened the door to see if the alarm had re-armed itself automatically and found that it had not. Making sure that he had not hit the button he handed the keys to me to hold out open handed in front of the group. A little flustered I asked the next question. "We left the gate open last time we were here... If you want us to close the gate when we leave, make the car go twice." Immediately the lights on the car flashed again and we heard the door locks click shut. Nervously Ashton tried the door and it was, in fact, locked. The keys had not left our sight. Still sure that it had to be a malfunction, Ashton took the keys from me. He unlocked the door, started the car and then shut it off again to reset the system, which seemed to end the malfunction and all activity for the night.

It wasn't until we reviewed the audio that any of us would be convinced that anything paranormal had happened at all. It was during the EVP session by the car that we found a jarring EVP. Immediately after I ask if we should close the gate a strange electrical sound can be heard on the recording directly preceding the loud click of the door locks. Ashton immediately identified the sound as a RF signal from the remote even though no keys were being pressed. While that was interesting, it wasn't that part of the audio that caught our attention. Immediately after the doors locked a deep, guttural, and forceful voice can be clearly heard and understood responding to us saying *Go back now.*

Listening to the recording still gives me chills even now. For the first time in all our investigations I felt like we were hearing the actual voice of whatever was there for the first time. In all previous recordings voices would sound human and lighter. This sounded, for lack of a better description, malevolent. If we had heard the response, at the time, we would have left immediately. But, other than the car going off, nothing else seemed to happen that night. We returned several times over the course of the next year with lackluster results. After the night of the car alarm incident it really seemed like all activity had completely vanished. Some of us theorized that maybe whatever was there had just grown bored with us, or maybe even left the location.

It was sometime after this that Allie told us about the recurring nightmare that she had started having about the cemetery. In it, we were on the Kyle investigation and she was watching static cameras in the back of the car. Out of the darkness only inches from her she saw the white face emerge. It was so close and so vivid she could see all the detail of its black glossy eyes, long black hair, and the cracking thick white paint that covers its face. The shape of it was distinctly human, but the features just seemed wrong and disproportionate. As she opened her mouth to scream so did the creature. The sound that came out was her voice, but it did not come from her mouth. It came from the face in the darkness. It was a chilling story that set the mood. I don't really believe in true premonition, but it had a lot of relevance to what was going on and what we were about to do. It seemed like every time we were going to Kyle one of us would take a piece of it home with us for a while.

In April of 2017 we decided that we would do one last official investigation to wrap up our case. We did several experiments to double check our baselines. I walked behind the fence line wearing a body camera while the group filmed me with a thermal camera from the other side. Even walking back as far as fifty yards I could easily be spotted moving around through the trees, putting to rest the argument that and animal could have hidden from the thermal camera back there. We stomped around trying to recreate the footsteps and animal galloping noises and could not come to a reasonable conclusion. The ground is simply too soft to make the types of sounds that we had all experienced. We deliberately set off the car alarm with the remote trying to recapture the RF signal, but it never came through the recorder again. Ashton conducted several test sessions trying to deliberately contaminate EVP recordings by talking at different distances and levels to try and prove that our recordings were nothing more than us being idiots. Everything we could think of, as well as, suggestions from people online we tried. Everything we did only made the argument in my head stronger that I we had not lost our minds for a year.

As we were wrapping up what would be our final investigation, we announced to Kyle that this would be the last time doing this. We told it that this was its last chance to make it's point. We didn't expect much since we hadn't captured a single event in five investigations. But, to our surprise we did get one last experience that would cement the location in my mind forever. As Allie and I were doing our last EVP session by the back area, Ashton had walked away to check some equipment. When we finished our last question, we turned to tell him that we were done and moving on. Oddly he was standing off in the shadows by a well-known grave, just standing and staring at us, merely a silhouette. Allie shouted out to him to tell him we were done and at that moment his figure moved behind the nearby tree. Ashton, answering Allies call, stepped out from behind the car which was parked on the opposite side of the graveyard.

Startled we ran back to the car and explained what just happened to Ashton who was confused. He said he had just seen something strange out of the corner of his eye while checking the feeds at the back of the car in another location. Looking all around we confirmed that we were the only ones there. We even checked to make sure he was not casting a shadow somehow. We could not recreate the effect. We packed our equipment and left the cemetery for the last time.

It took us eight months to go through every bit of footage and audio that we had collected over the course of a year. We even found new evidence in our original footage after knowing what to look for. Of all the investigations we have been on, this is the only place that truly leaves me with a feeling long after we have left. I can't say I believe the area is haunted. But, I can say there is *something* there that affects all of us that I can't explain. Ashton has said that he does not want to investigate the location officially anymore, much less go back. Allie still has nightmares and the rest of the group have their reservations. Even just writing about our experiences makes me feel like I'm being watched. But, it's still my favorite place and I know eventually I will go back, with or without my team.

OBJECTIVE BELIEF

Often, when I say to someone that science has not produced any data proving the existence of the supernatural, I am met with a reply that science has not produced enough evidence ruling it out. But, it's not the burden of science to disprove the existence of the paranormal. It is the burden of those who believe in it to prove its validity. Science, in a nutshell is a mixed bag, in that, very often when the process is followed we either don't get the answer to the question we were asking in the first place or, even more frequently, we find the answers to questions we didn't even know to ask. When NASA completed the Apollo missions not only did we answer the question *could humans safely travel to the moon and back,* we also found that life before microwave ovens, Velcro, and Tang™ was simply barbaric. It's the nature of science to be objective, but it would be hard to prove a theory if you didn't also believe what you were trying to prove at least to the extent of testing it. It seems like every time I discuss that science has not yet proven the existence of the paranormal that I get told I do not believe, or I am called a skeptic in vein. While I am skeptical of most claims, I do in fact, believe in the existence of paranormal phenomenon. My body of work's sole purpose is to *prove* the existence of these events. However, to do that I have to remain objective to the data at all costs for it to be valid. I have what I like to call an objective belief in the paranormal.

So many people are drawn to and interested in the paranormal. What is the allure that keeps the topics and ideas alive in the face of so much skeptic insistence from the scientific community? It must be something encoded into the human condition that makes us all want to see past what is seeable. As time goes on, and I get older, this truth becomes more and more evident every day. For hundreds of years we have all known it to be a truth that the Earth is a globe, spinning around a sun, that is a vast network of other bodies in the universe. However, 2016 saw the biggest rise in flat earthers than any previous year since anyone has ever bothered to count. Although there are staggering levels of scientific documentation to back up the fact that our planet is 4.54 billion years old, there are still some who choose to ignore those facts and swear that it is only six-thousand years old. Even in the face of facts, people will let their beliefs outweigh what is right in front of them. This is most evident in our residentially contracted cases.

NTPI conducts full scientific investigations at many different types of public locations to determine if there is any practical evidence to be collected. We have an ethical responsibility to present facts about what we find honestly and in an objective manner. However, the most difficult types of locations to investigate involves delving deeper into private homes at the request of the residents. In these cases, clients claim to have experienced something paranormal in the one place that should feel safe and comforting. It's not only a possible paranormal event, but something deeply personal and sometimes guarded. In these cases, we will attempt to study the residence and subjects, objectively collect data, debunk all instances where natural and explainable events could be mistaken for supernatural phenomenon, and help put their mind at ease however we can. However, sometimes it's not as simple as offering a logical explanation.

While we would never lie to a client about what's going on in their home, we have an obligation be sensitive to their feelings about the results. Through a great many errors, we have found that some people are not as interested in the facts of a case as they are having their experiences validated. A common misconception about the debunking process is that just because we discover that an experience isn't paranormal, doesn't mean that we are saying the experiences were any less real. There is still a very tactile experience to be dealt with and we simply want to explain the mechanism by which those experiences came to be. Ultimately, it's up to the client to decide what that means to them personally. They might feel that we're somehow invalidating what they've been through, and may feel apprehensive after we present an explanation, causing them to be defensive. From a psychological standpoint, it's my evaluation that, if an experience in your life no longer has meaning just because it happened through the means of an explainable mechanic, what does that really say about your belief and faith in spiritual matters?

Whatever questions those actions bring up philosophically are technically outside of the scope of what we have personally set out to accomplish. In the end, our goal is to document facts objectively, and not speculate the higher purpose of what caused them. We have learned over the course of several investigations to actively gauge what kind of answer clients are looking for and are willing to accept to navigate these very awkward social, and somehow businesslike, situations. It's is a problem that I feel many paranormal investigators face when dealing with clients, and often are put under pressure to produce a watered-down result that implies a paranormal element even if one doesn't exist. It's this practice that can sometimes give a perfectly sound investigator a seemingly shady reputation, causing a slew of other issues down the road. In my career as an investigator I've caused myself a lot of undue stress to navigate those waters without compromising my integrity.

In this this job, I have never positively confirmed to a client that their house was haunted. At most, that their location had some incidents of inconclusive data we could not resolve. Usually, we will present a few theories as to what may have caused the incident based on available evidence, in which one of the possibilities may *sometimes* include paranormal activity. We may even go as far as suggesting that we feel the evidence supports a good *probability* of paranormal activity if appropriate. But, ultimately the interpretation is up to the client to decide and there's very little we can do about that. It can be very frustrating to tell clients a laundry list of reasons that we don't feel there is anything going on, only to have them hold on to the one shred of inconclusive data and swear they're living in a haunted house. It's a frustration I try not to voice to often, but there none the less. There is no current amount of evidence we can supply to say a location is positively haunted. Once again, there simply is no proof. How could I look a client in the eye and tell them beyond the shadow of a doubt that there is paranormal activity in their home? How would I feel months down the line when during a remodel they uncover a faulty water pipe that we couldn't detect that was the source of the sounds being made? I'm pretty sure both the client and myself will feel extremely stupid when that missed pipe turns out to have caused thousands of dollars in property damage. Without proof we simply cannot know for sure, and I feel we have an ethical responsibility to tell the clients the truth. Not just what they want to hear, and that goes both ways.

Belief can be an unstoppable force. If they are deep-seated, there is really no way to convince a person that they might be wrong. In fact, trying to prove that their beliefs are simply misinterpretations of the facts, or an overactive imagination, may lead to even more defense and further belief in whatever it is. Although substantial scientific evidence can be used to debunk many claims in cases, a client may not want to hear that their wiring is bad, or that low hanging power lines are causing an EMF readout off the scales, which might be causing feelings of paranoia and hallucinations. If someone truly, wholeheartedly, believes that there is a spirit living in their home, it doesn't matter how much proof you present to the contrary. After we are done with the investigation, they will continue to believe it was all a ghost and likely tell their friends that we confirmed it.

But, however stubborn belief can make a person, there have been positive aspects to it that cannot be denied. Without belief in the supernatural, many people would never be able to move through the grieving process of losing loved ones. Many time the belief in something beyond ourselves helps people to move on and heal. A belief in a higher power has been known to give people the ability to make it through sickness, anxiety and addiction. Studies on the placebo effect have proven time and again that just really believing that a medicine is going to help you can produce the same result as actually taking the drug. If a mindset can change the physiology of your body, could it possibly manipulate the world around you? Could the power of belief trick you into thinking that you were experiencing a paranormal event? Stranger still, could a strong belief manifest paranormal activity? Two separate studies suggest that either of these scenarios could be possible.

THE PHILIP EXPERIMENT

In 1972, mathematician A. R. G. Owen and psychologist Dr. Joel Whitton, created and supervised an experiment that would later be known as the *Philip Experiment*. Conducted in Ontario, the purpose of the experiments was to determine if subjects could communicate with and manifest fictionalized ghosts through the expectations belief.

For the experiment, Owen and Whitton, created a fictional character through laborious and purposeful methodology. The character created and agreed upon was named "Philip Aylesford", who was simply called Philip during the test. His fictional history coincided with actual events and places, but also was laced with multiple contradictions and errors. The created character was born in 1624 in England, had an early military career and was knighted by the age of sixteen for his heroic acts of bravery. Philip was a soldier in the English Civil War and eventually became personal friends with Charles II, and began working for him as a spy. Philip was unhappily married to a woman named Dorothea and later fell in love with a Gypsy girl who was accused of witchcraft and burned at the stake. In despair, Philip committed suicide in 1654 at the age of thirty.

The group was carefully selected by Whitton and made up primarily of people he knew to be skeptical of the paranormal. The test group consisted of A. R. G.'s wife Iris Owen, former chairperson of MENSA in Canada Margaret Sparrows, industrial designer Andy H., his wife Lorne, heating engineer Al Peacock, accountant Bernice M, bookkeeper Dorothy O'Donnell, and sociology student Sidney K. None of the participants claimed to be psychic mediums in any sense of the word and had at least a marginally skeptical view of the practice of séances.

The participants were seated around a table and asked to contact the spirit of Philip. With initial séances yielding no contact, no communication, and no phenomenon, Owen changed test conditions one by one. By dimming lights and changing the environment to mimic that of a more "traditional" séance, Participants began feeling a presence. Table vibrations, breezes, unexplained echoes, and rapping sounds which matched responses to questions about Philip's life became more frequent in the sessions. Finally, the group was able to conjure a manifestation in the form of poltergeist activity causing the table to move and eventually tilt up onto one leg. However, once the control group knew that the character was fictional, as suddenly as the activity came on it disappeared.

The experiment was criticized for lacking solid controls and providing ambiguous results due to the unreliability of séances. Other groups repeated the tests, which created fictional characters named "Lilith" and "Humphrey", yielded similar results under similar circumstances and were ultimately deemed inconclusive. Overseeing psychologist Joel Whitton concluded that the effects were produced by participants as a subconscious defense mechanism, causing their behavior to regress to a childlike mentality.

There have been arguments made on both sides of the case. However, it is of considerable note that the results of the experiment were repeatable to a certain degree. So, while we cannot rule the findings as scientific certainty, the study does make some rather interesting arguments. Namely, that not only can we psychologically convince ourselves as a group of things that we openly are skeptical about, but we could *possibly* have the ability to physically manifest those fantasies as well. Some mediums would argue that the group had contacted a spirit that was imitating the character that the groups were trying to contact. Others would suggest that members of the group were hoaxing and influencing the rest of the group. In any case we can all agree that deep rooted subconscious belief in the paranormal at the very least does have an influence over the outcome of people looking to contact those things.

THE "FOP" SENSORY EXPERIMENT

In more recent years, a separate and more technological approach was taken to a similar idea. Professor Olaf Blanke, from the Ecole Polytechnique Federale de Lausanne (EPFL) in Switzerland theorizes that spectral and paranormal encounters are simply the result of overloaded and confused sensory input. Scientists, like Blanke, have suspected that ghosts and a *"Feeling of Presence"* are no more than an illusion created by the mind. It's been well noted that patients who suffer from neurological, psychiatric conditions, or experiencing extreme physical or emotional pain frequently report paranormal phenomenon. Balnke set out to prove that ghosts are no more than an event created by the mind when it momentarily loses track of the body's location due to illness, exertion or stress.

In the experiment lab technicians set up a robotic control device that allows volunteers to control the movements of a jointed mechanical arm with their index fingers. The movements of the sensory deprived test subjects were relayed to the arm behind them which touched their backs and created a tactile sensation that was in sync with their own movements.

When both the finger-pushing and back-touching occurred at the same time, it created the illusion that the volunteers were caressing their own backs. Most reported the sensation as strange but not at all unnerving or unpleasant. However, when the back-touching was delayed and 500 milliseconds out of sync with the finger movements, the volunteers suddenly felt as if they were being watched, and touched, by one or more spectral beings in the room. During this time, the subjects also reported having the sensation of drifting backwards, towards the unseen hand.

When questioned, several reported a strong feeling of invisible people being close to them. On average, they counted two, with up to four being reported. Of the 12 healthy participants, two were so disturbed by the experience that they asked the scientists to end the experiment which ultimately caused panic attacks.

Olaf Blanke, in an interview with the Telegraph, stated: "Our experiment induced the sensation of a foreign presence in the laboratory for the first time. It shows that it can arise under normal conditions, simply through conflicting sensory-motor signals... This confirms that it is caused by an altered perception of their own bodies in the brain." In his paper Blanke along with co-author Dr Giulio Rognini tell us that: "Our brain possesses several representations of our body in space. Under normal conditions, it can assemble a unified self-perception of the self from these representations. But, when the system malfunctions because of disease or, in this case a robot, this can sometimes create a second representation of one's own body, which is no longer perceived as 'me' but as someone else, a 'presence'." The experiment suggests that "feelings of presence" (FOPs), often interpreted as spirits, angels or demons, and are really all in the mind.

In the full report, the researchers describe the case of mountaineer, Reinhold Messner, who had an FOP experience while descending from the summit of the Himalayan peak Nanga Parbat in June 1970. Accompanied by his brother, he was freezing, exhausted and oxygen-starved. He recalled becoming aware of a third climber "descending with us, keeping a regular distance, a little to my right and a few steps away from me, just outside my field of vision".

Also as part of the experiment, the researchers carried out brain scans of 12 patients with neurological disorders who had encountered FOPs in the past. They identified disturbances in three brain regions, the insular cortex, parietal-frontal cortex, and temporo-parietal cortex. All were involved in self-awareness, movement, and sense of position in space. The research was published in the journal Current Biology.

Thinking about these two experiments: How did it make you

feel? Do you think you could objectively gauge where you fall into the scheme of thinking about the paranormal? If reading about each case study convinced you that science once again proved that paranormal events are nothing more than the mind playing tricks on you, than you probably fall into some category of skeptic. If reading the results of the studies upset you because you felt like the studies didn't allow for certain variables that would help an argument for paranormal phenomenon, you're very much a believer. But, if you fall anywhere into the gray area of people who think that while the experiments were valid and produced good results, could benefit from more study and research into other variables, you might be an *objective believer.*

It's my opinion that people are desperate to find a connection to the world in a way that makes them unique in it. In a world where technology is taking over and almost no corner remains undiscovered, I too find myself relating to this idea. Why do I study the paranormal? Sure, I could say it's because my experience inspired me to delve deeper into the unknown. But, that is precisely my point. It's the unknown that is the allure. It makes me special. It gives me that something to learn about, different from others, that sets me apart from the pack and helps me to reconnect in a way that makes me feel a sense of discovery that seems out of reach to so many others. And, that's what everyone else is looking for as well. The unknown something that can only be taken away by greater understanding of the world around us. To work in the unknowable, you give yourself free license to imagine, discover, and invent. But, to that extent, you also can cause great damage. Religion and faith should be a beautiful thing, pure and full of good intentions. But, look at the turmoil it has caused since its first inception. When we start explaining the mechanics of how these things come to be, the instinct of the person is to cling to the ideas that these things are unknowable. It's a deeply ingrained defense mechanism in the human psyche to not upset the pack for survival. But, this is an instinct that even I myself must fight to remain objective.

For me, knowing a thing only makes it that much greater. For me, knowing that there are supernatural things at work that operate within the same physical confines of our physical laws and reality is a great comfort and only strengthens my belief in it. It's not my goal to tell people that these things aren't real. My goal is to absolutely prove these things are real and that they can exist in the reality we have come to understand. Even if that means we must expand our understanding of reality to include the things the we previously did not understand. There is no amount of evidence that I can present that will make an acceptable substitute for proof. At the end, when everything is said and done, our belief and your belief in the paranormal is still just a guess. But, hopefully, with enough evidence we can make a uniquely informed speculation about the things that exist out there. And maybe one day, we will have the proof we need either way.

ABOUT THE AUTHOR

Born and raised in Fort Worth, Texas. Ashton Rogers is the lead investigator for NTParanormal Investigations research team. After having his first personal experience with the paranormal in 2013, with the support of his friends, started the NTParanormal Investigations group. Since then they have been chasing down and investigating reports of paranormal activity wherever they could it and adding new members along the way. In addition to being a paranormal investigator, Ashton is an accomplished writer. He has published several sci-fi / horror based short stories, contributed to independent screenplays, and is a syndicated author for multiple paranormal websites. Outside of writing, Ashton is also a musician, photographer, and game designer.

You can find more work by Ashton Rogers at
www.amazon.com/Ashton-Rogers

Made in the USA
Middletown, DE
06 February 2018